GUITAR ROADS

A Beginner's Guide to the Guitar

Andrew Cooper

Copyright © 2014 by Guitar Roads LLC

Photos and Design by Wendolyn Deal

Photo Editing: Photo Wonder

Edited by Teresa Leigh Ander and Louise Hawker

Guitar Roads books are available at discounted rates when purchased in bulk for resale. For details, contact:

Guitar Roads LLC, PO Box 1624, Bend, OR 97709

or info@guitarroads.com

Printed in the United States

ISBN: 978-0-9915492-0-7

To view and download the lesson videos go to:
GuitarRoads.com/book-downloads

CONTENTS

4 ACKNOWLEDGMENTS
5 INTRODUCTION

Part One: Essential Concepts

LESSON 1
GETTING STARTED   8
8   TYPES OF GUITARS
9   PARTS OF THE ACOUSTIC GUITAR
10 PARTS OF THE ELECTRIC GUITAR
11 HOLDING THE GUITAR
12 HOLDING THE PICK
13 FINGER PLACEMENT
14 HOW TO TUNE THE GUITAR
16 HOW TO READ TABLATURE
17 CHORD DIAGRAMS

LESSON 2
PLAYING IN TIME   18
18 READING RHYTHM SLASHES
19 MAJOR AND MINOR CHORDS
20 STRUMMING IN TIME

LESSON 3
PLAYING SINGLE NOTES   22
22 READING TAB RHYTHMS
24 FRETTED NOTES
25 THE MAJOR SCALE
26 HOW TO PLAY A MELODY

LESSON 4
PICKING DEVELOPMENT   28
28 ARPEGGIOS
30 ALTERNATE PICKING

LESSON 5
POWER CHORDS   32
32 TWO-NOTE POWER CHORDS

LESSON 6
BLUES BASICS   34
34 COMPING PATTERNS
36 PLAYING A SHUFFLE

LESSON 7
PLAYING A RIFF   38
38 SINGLE-NOTE RIFFS

LESSON 8
POWER CHORD RIFFS   40
40 THREE-NOTE POWER CHORDS
41 READING RESTS AND TIES
42 POWER CHORDS AND SINGLE-NOTES
43 STRING BENDING

Part Two: Chords & Rhythm

LESSON 9
OPEN CHORDS   46
46 OPEN-POSITION MAJOR CHORDS
48 OPEN-POSITION MINOR CHORDS

LESSON 10
CHORD SWITCHING   50
50 COMMON CHORD CHANGES

LESSON 11
CHORD PROGRESSIONS   54
54 MAJOR CHORD PROGRESSIONS
57 MINOR CHORD PROGRESSIONS

LESSON 12
STRUM PATTERNS 58
58 GAINING RHYTHMIC CONTROL
60 THE SYNCOPATED STRUM
61 SIXTEENTH NOTE STRUMS

LESSON 13
SEVENTH CHORDS 62
62 DOMINANT SEVENTH CHORDS
64 THE 12 BAR BLUES PROGRESSION

LESSON 14
CHORDAL TECHNIQUES 66
66 PICKING PATTERNS
68 THE BASS STRUM
69 HAMMER-ONS AND PULL-OFFS

Part Three: Moving Up The Fretboard

LESSON 15
MOVEABLE CHORDS 72
72 SIXTH-STRING-ROOT POWER CHORDS
75 FIFTH-STRING-ROOT POWER CHORDS
77 COMBINING SIXTH AND FIFTH-STRING ROOT POWER CHORDS

LESSON 16
RIFFING TECHNIQUES 78
78 PALM MUTING
79 PEDAL TONES
80 SLIDES
81 GALLOP RHYTHMS

LESSON 17
ESSENTIAL BLUES RIFFS 82
82 TURNAROUNDS
84 THE BLUES BOOGIE
85 HOW TO PLAY A MOVEABLE BLUES PROGRESSION

LESSON 18
BARRE CHORDS 88
88 SIXTH-STRING-ROOT MAJOR AND MINOR BARRE CHORDS
90 FIFTH-STRING-ROOT MAJOR AND MINOR BARRE CHORDS
92 SIXTH AND FIFTH-STRING-ROOT BARRED SEVENTH CHORDS

LESSON 19
CHORD FAMILIES 94
94 DIATONIC CHORDS
95 POPULAR CHORD PROGRESSIONS

LESSON 20
GUITAR SOLOS 100
100 E MINOR PENTATONIC SCALE
101 PHRASING
102 ARTICULATION
103 THE PENTATONIC BOX PATTERN
104 VIBRATO
105 REPEATED LICKS

Part Four: Helpful Resources

108 FRETBOARD DIRECTORY
109 STRUM PATTERNS
110 KEY CHART
111 CHORD CONSTRUCTION
112 GLOSSARY
114 BLANK TAB
115 BLANK CHORD DIAGRAMS
116 NOTATION LEGEND

ACKNOWLEDGMENTS

MY FAMILY, ESPECIALLY my wife, for all of her love and support; as well as my parents, who have been there since the beginning; Ted Engstrom for his early endorsement of my teaching skills; Lino Allesio for his technical assistance; and of course my students who have been some of my greatest teachers!

PHOTO CREDITS

INTRODUCTION

ANYBODY CAN PLAY THE GUITAR! Unfortunately, many would-be guitar players give up early, buying into the myth that they lack musical "talent." This is usually the result of a poor learning experience brought on by a teacher or book that fails to take into account the psychology of the beginning guitar student. There are many physical, mental, and emotional barriers that beginning guitarists have to overcome in order to make music by pressing metal against wood. Though there is no real "right way" to learn or teach the guitar, there are methods that can shorten the learning curve. Therefore, many of the lessons in this book are organized into short, simple concepts that are practical and applicable to most styles of music. Not every musical concept or theory is covered in great detail or at all, as it is my belief that much of this is on a need to know basis and in the beginning you just don't need to know. These "front loaded" theory methods, as I call them, explain away everything before you've even have had a chance to play anything, resulting in more confusion. All of that aside, remember that what you put in you will get out, and every great guitar player achieved their level of prowess not by divine intervention but through dedicated practice. Some things will come easier than others and everybody learns at a different pace. Enjoy!

ABOUT THE AUTHOR

ANDREW COOPER is a professional musician and educator located in Bend, OR. Classically trained, Andrew has helped hundreds of students overcome the hurdles of learning how to play the guitar in the past 10 years. When not teaching, he performs extensively throughout the Northwest both as a solo performer (www.andrewcoopermusic.com) and with fellow guitarist Lino Alessio.

PART ONE

ESSENTIAL
CONCEPTS

LESSON 1

GETTING STARTED

The modern guitar, as we know it today, was developed in Spain in the mid to late 19th century. Generally looked down upon by the music public of the time, it was through the efforts of Spanish performers and composers, most notably Andrés Segovia, that the guitar continues in popularity.

TYPES OF GUITARS

GUITARS CAN BE CATEGORIZED into two main types: acoustic and electric. There are two types of acoustic guitar: classical and steel-string. *Classical guitars* use nylon strings which have a softer, warmer sound. The modern *steel-string acoustic*, as the name implies, uses steel strings that create a brighter tone and additional volume. The *electric guitar* also uses steel strings that are then amplified through the use of electronic pickups, creating even more volume and an endless world of tonal possibilities.

CLASSICAL

STEEL-STRING

ELECTRIC

PARTS OF THE ACOUSTIC GUITAR

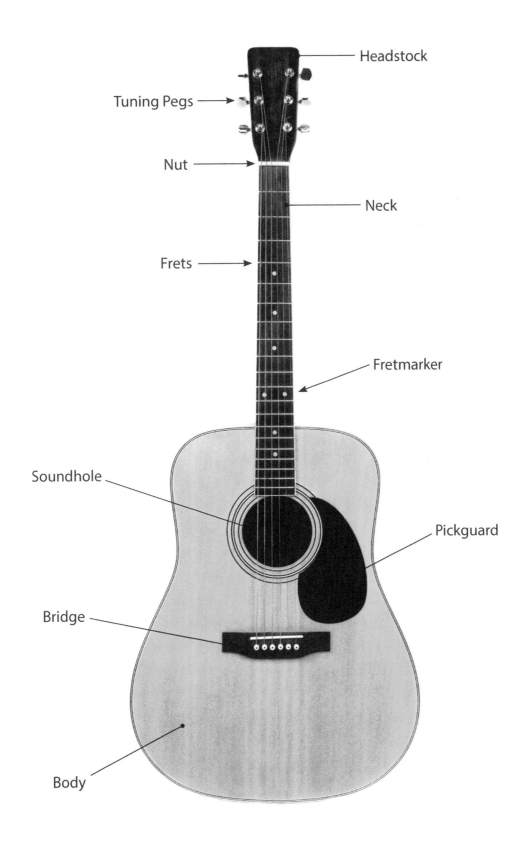

PARTS OF THE ELECTRIC GUITAR

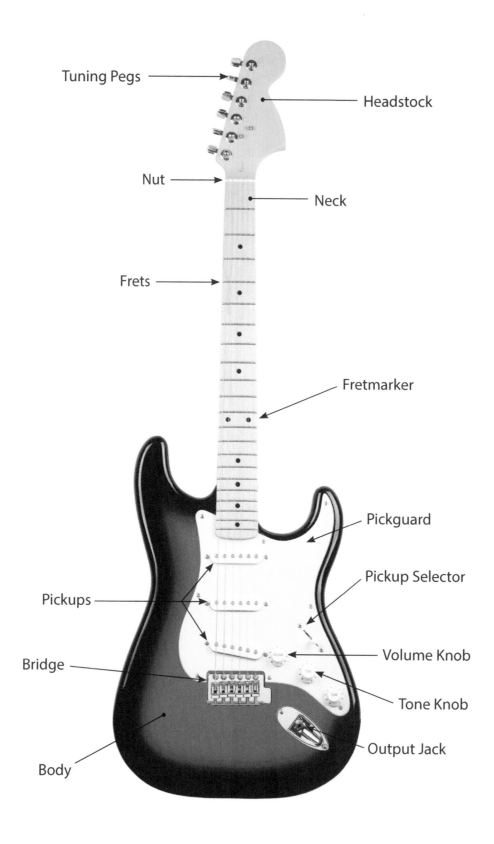

Tuning Pegs

Headstock

Nut

Neck

Frets

Fretmarker

Pickguard

Pickup Selector

Pickups

Volume Knob

Bridge

Tone Knob

Output Jack

Body

HOLDING THE GUITAR

WHETHER YOU ARE SITTING OR STANDING, make sure that you adopt a posture that is both comfortable and allows you to see both hands. When standing, adjust the strap to a height that allows you reach all of the strings. When sitting, rest the guitar on your right leg or you can also use a footstool for better posture.

CASUAL

CLASSICAL

HOLDING THE PICK

THE PICK SHOULD BE HELD between your index finger and thumb (like giving the "OK" sign) with the tip pointed toward the guitar. You want to hold the pick tight enough so that you don't drop it, but not too tight so that it creates extra tension.

FINGER PLACEMENT

YOUR FINGERS SHOULD BE PLACED halfway or more in the space between the fret wires and are numbered 1 through 4.

THE THUMB SHOULD stay up (I call it "give the audience the thumbs up") which stabilizes the hand and also makes it easier to press down on the string(s).

HOW TO TUNE THE GUITAR

TUNING THE GUITAR is important and something that should be done every time you pick up your guitar. The most common tuning is called *standard tuning*, whereby the strings are tuned from the sixth (thickest) string to the 1st (thinnest) string to the notes EADGBE. The thickest string is sometimes referred to as the "Low E" and thinnest string as the "High E". You can tune the guitar with an electronic tuner or by using the other guitar strings (**FIGURE 1**).

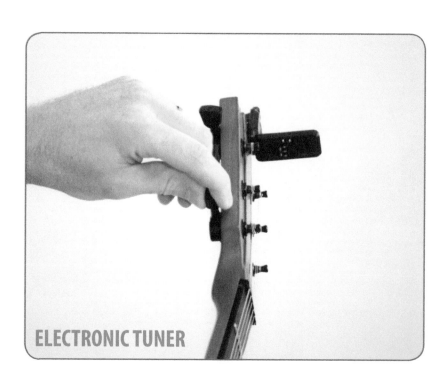

ELECTRONIC TUNER

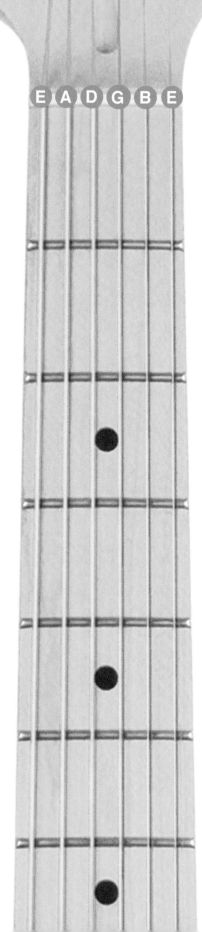

E A D G B E

Figure 1 - *Tuning*

6th String - Open E Adjust the tuning peg until the pitch matches the pitch of the reference note from a electronic tuner, piano, or pitch pipe.

5th String - Open A Press your finger on the fifth fret of the low E string. Pluck both strings until the A string matches the pitch of the pressed string.

4th String - Open D Press your finger on the fifth fret of the A string. Pluck both strings until the D string matches the pitch of the pressed string.

3rd String - Open G Press your finger on the fifth fret of the D string. Pluck both strings until the G string matches the pitch of the pressed string.

2nd String - Open B Press your finger on the fourth fret of the G string. Pluck both strings until the B string matches the pitch of the pressed string.

1st String - Open E Press your finger on the fifth fret of the B string. Pluck both strings until the E string matches the pitch of the pressed string.

HOW TO READ TABLATURE

TABLATURE OR TAB is a notation system for stringed instruments that shows you where to place your fingers on the strings. Notice that there are six lines in the example below, with each representing a string on the guitar. The "0" indicates that the string is plucked open or unfretted. Numbers (1,2,3,4,etc.) represent the frets, showing you which fret to press down on and on which string.

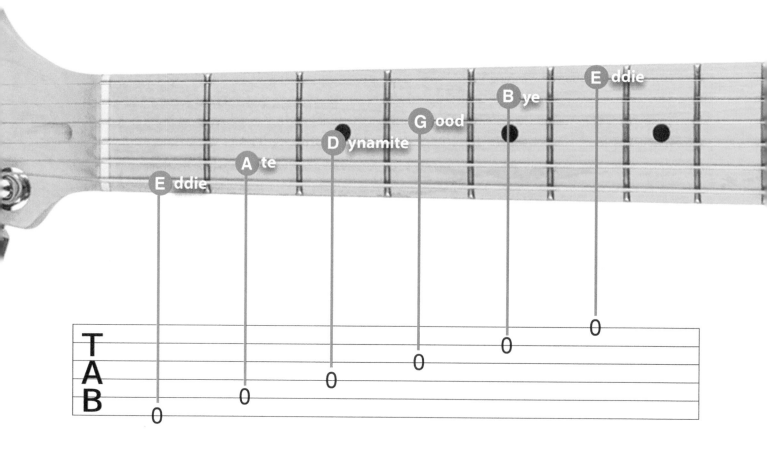

CHORD DIAGRAMS

CHORD DIAGRAMS are graphical illustrations of where to place your fingers on the fretboard. Each of the vertical lines represents a guitar string, with the thickest string on the left side. The horizontal lines are the frets, with dots to show you where to place your fingers.

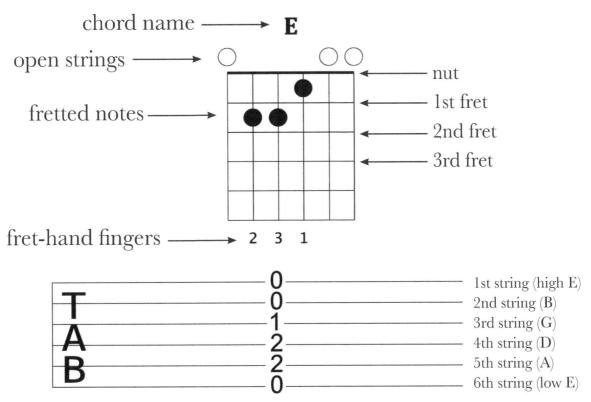

LESSON 2
PLAYING IN TIME

Knowing how to play in time is one of the most important first steps when learning any musical instrument. The tempo and rhythm act as a framework that gives a song its basic structure. In this lesson, you'll learn how to strum some basic chords to a specific pattern of beats by reading rhythm slashes.

READING RHYTHM SLASHES

MUSIC NOTATION IS DIVIDED into what are called *measures* (also referred to as *bars*). Each measure gets a certain number of beats depending on the *time signature*. In the example below (**FIGURE 2**), the time signature is 4/4 indicating that there are four beats per measure. Each measure contains a rhythm slash which tells you when to strum and how long to hold the chord.

Figure 2 - *Rhythm Slashes*

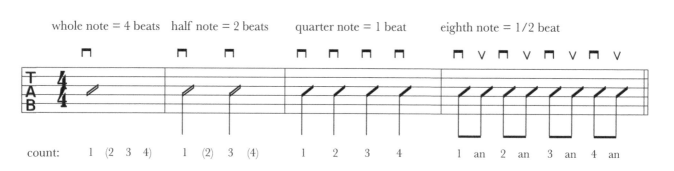

MAJOR AND MINOR CHORDS

A CHORD IS A GROUP OF NOTES that are sounded together. There are many different types of chords, but most are categorized as being either a *major chord* or a *minor chord*. Think of major chords as sounding "happy" or "lighter" and minor chords as sounding "sad" or "darker." Major chords are written with just the letter (E Major: E) and minor chords are written with a lower case "m" next to the chord letter (E minor: Em). Strum the chords (**FIGURE 3**) in a downward motion across all six strings listening to how the sound changes when you press and release your index finger.

Figure 3 - *E major and E minor*

STRUMMING IN TIME

THE FOLLOWING EXERCISES combine the E and Em chords with the rhythm slashes you just learned (**Figures 4A-D**). As you strum the chords, be sure to count out loud "ONE-two-three-four" while tapping your foot on each count.

Figure 4a - *Whole notes (4 beats)*

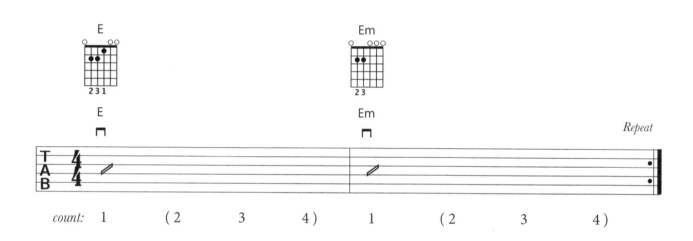

count: 1   (2   3   4)   1   (2   3   4)

PRACTICE TIP!

How to Strum Properly

■ The motion should come mostly from the wrist giving you greater control. Each strum should stay within 2-3 inches from either the low or high strings.

Figure 4b - *Half notes (2 beats)*

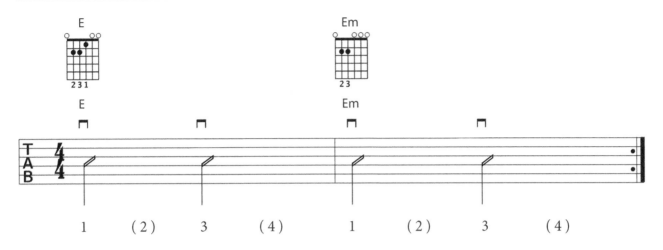

Figure 4c - *Quarter notes (1 beat)*

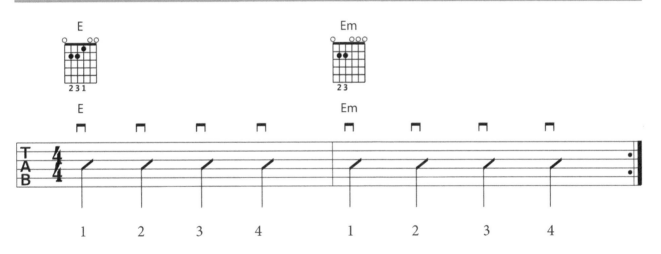

Figure 4d - *Eighth notes (1/2 beat)*

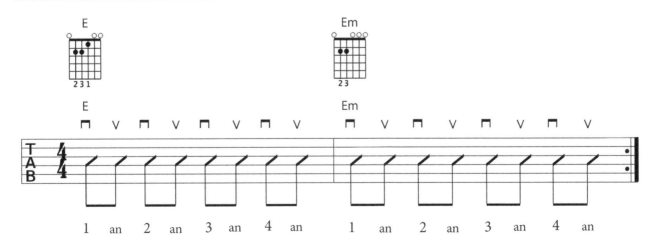

LESSON 3
PLAYING SINGLE NOTES

Now that you're familiar with how rhythm works, we'll apply the same concepts to single-notes in TABLATURE. First we'll begin by understanding how to read rhythms in TAB before moving on to your first scale patterns and melodies.

READING TAB RHYTHMS

TABLATURE OR **TAB,** is one of the most common ways that guitar music is transcribed. TAB dates back to the Renaissance and Baroque eras and was used for many lute and vihuela pieces. As was mentioned in Lesson 1, each line represents a guitar string with the top line representing the high E (thinnest string). A zero on the string line indicates that the string is plucked open; i.e., plucking it without pressing your fingers down on the fret. A number on the string tells which fret to place your finger on. Just like the rhythm slashes, the stems underneath indicate the number of beats for each note (**FIGURE 5**).

Figure 5 - *TAB rhythms*

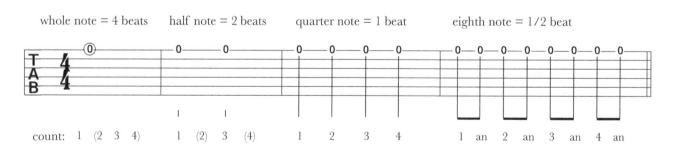

STARTING ON THE low E string, pluck each string using quarter notes, making sure that you do not strike any adjacent strings (**FIGURE 6A**). After you become comfortable with the string changes in **FIGURES 6B-C**, avoid looking at the picking hand and try to visualize where the strings are located.

Figure 6a

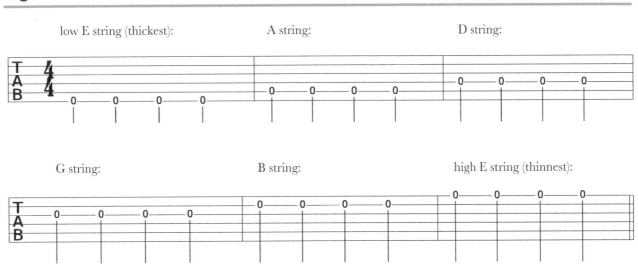

Figure 6b

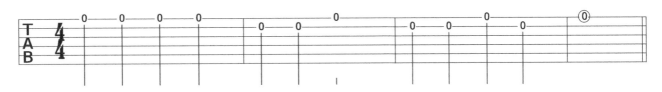

Figure 6c

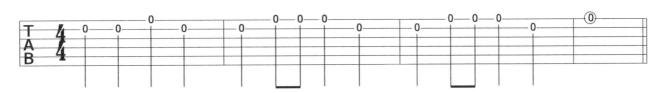

FRETTED NOTES

THERE ARE 12 EQUALLY spaced notes or pitches in the Western music system (see page 108 *Fretboard Directory*). Known as the *chromatic scale* from the Greek word "chroma" which means "to color," the notes of the music scale can be played on the guitar by starting on one fret and moving one fret at a time for twelve frets. The best way to approach single note patterns, especially when playing higher up on the fretboard, is to use position playing. A *position* is a fixed location on the fretboard and gets it's name from the fret that the first finger plays. For example, the fifth position would mean that the first finger plays the fifth fret, the second finger plays the sixth fret, third finger is on the seventh fret, and fourth finger plays the eighth fret. **FIGURES 7A-B** shows how position playing would be applied to the chromatic scale on the high E string.

Ascending **Descending**

Figure 7a - *Ascending*

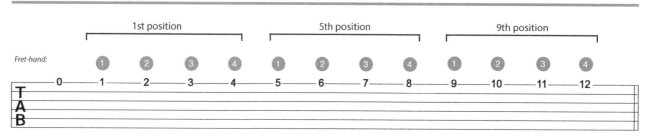

Figure 7b - *Descending*

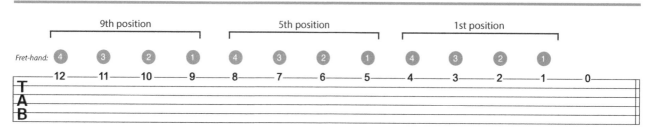

THE MAJOR SCALE

THERE ARE MANY different scales that are derived from the notes of the chromatic scale, each with its own particular sound and character. A scale, by definition, is a pattern of notes that can be played in ascending and descending order. The *major scale* may sound familiar, as it is the cornerstone which all Western music is based. Unique to the guitar are all the ways notes can be played or voiced, depending on the string and location on the fretboard. **FIGURES 8A-C** are a few examples of how the C Major scale can be played on the guitar using position playing.

Figure 8a

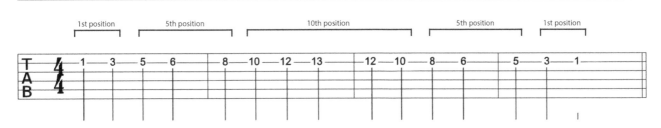

Figure 8b

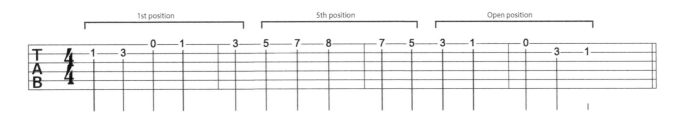

Figure 8c

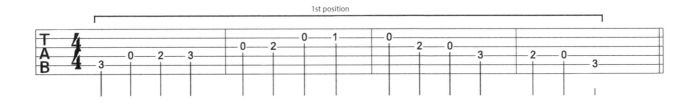

HOW TO PLAY A MELODY

Now that you're familiar with the sound and patterns of the C major scale, let's learn how to play a melody that uses these notes. A *melody* is simply a pattern of notes that is organized to express a theme or emotion. In **FIGURE 9**, we have the main melody from Beethoven's 9th symphony "Ode to Joy." Remember to pay attention to the fretting hand, making sure that you are using the correct fingers. The 1st finger (index) is assigned to the first fret, while the 3rd (ring) is assigned to the third fret.

Figure 9 - *Ode to Joy*

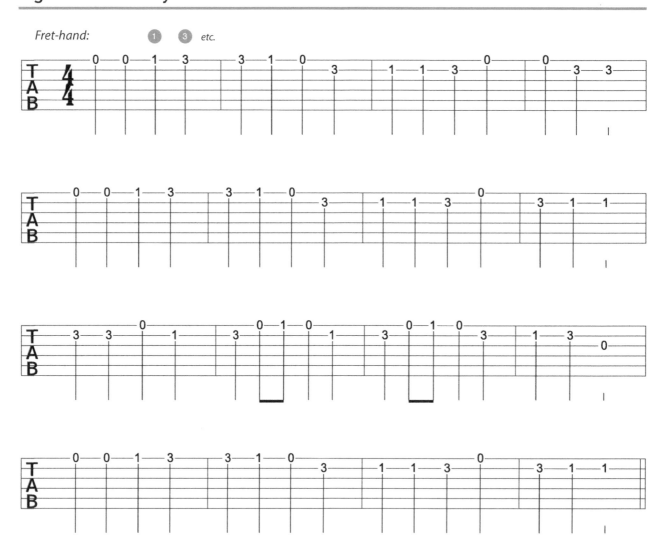

WORDS TO PLAY BY

"The guitar is a miniature orchestra in itself."

LUDWIG VAN BEETHOVEN

LESSON 4
PICKING DEVELOPMENT

So far we've looked at how to strum a chord and play a single-note melody. In this lesson we'll look at some other commonly used techniques, such as alternate picking and playing an arpeggio pattern.

ARPEGGIOS

IN ADDITION TO STRUMMING chords and playing melodies, you can also play what is called an *arpeggio* (ar-peh-jee-oh), an Italian word for "like a harp." This means that each note or string is played in a sequence, one after the other. The example in **FIGURE 10** shows the difference between strumming the strings and playing them as an arpeggio. **FIGURE 11** is an eighth-note arpeggio pattern played repeatedly on the top three strings, while the fretting hand moves up and down the high E string.

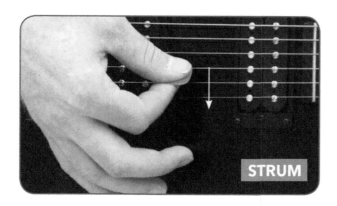

Figure 10

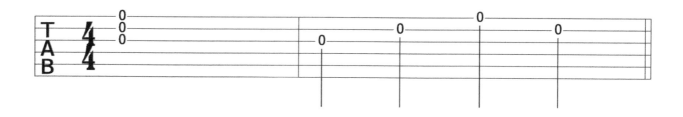

Figure 11

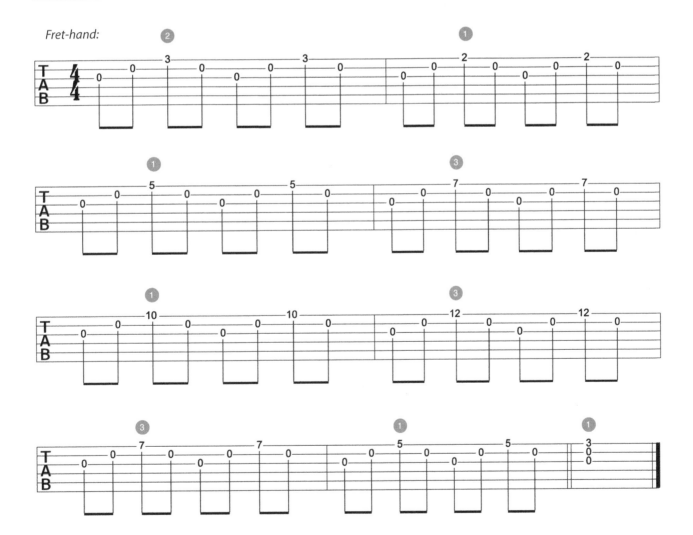

ALTERNATE PICKING

ALTERNATE PICKING is a technique that employs the use of alternating downstrokes and upstrokes for single-note passages. This can be helpful when attempting to play faster with minimal effort. **FIGURES 12A-B** are examples of two different alternate picking techniques that can be used when crossing strings: *outside picking* and *inside picking*.

OUTSIDE PICKING

INSIDE PICKING

Figure 12a - *Outside picking*

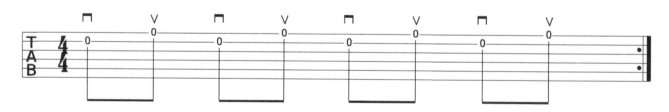

Figure 12b - *Inside picking*

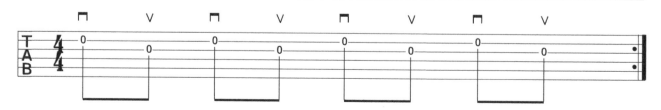

FIGURE 13 is a traditional Spanish piece called "Malaguena" that is played with a 3/4 time signature. This means that there are three beats per measure. Count out loud: "ONE-two-three" "ONE-two-three" As you play the arpeggio pattern, hold the partial chord shapes over each measure, paying close attention to the recommended picking pattern.

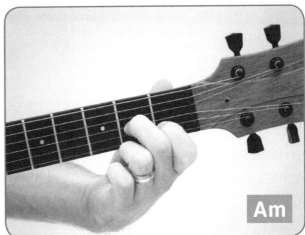

Figure 13 - *Malaguena*

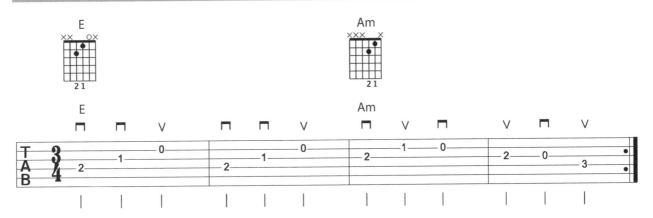

LESSON 5
POWER CHORDS

A staple of blues and rock, power chords can be heard in many popular rock songs such as "You Really Got Me" by The Kinks and "Smoke on the Water" by Deep Purple.

TWO-NOTE POWER CHORDS

NOTICE THAT EACH CHORD name in **FIGURE 14** corresponds with the open string. This is called the *root note* or the first note of a chord. A power chord is built from the root and fifth scale steps of a major scale and is also referred to as a "5" chord (see page 111 *Chord Construction*).

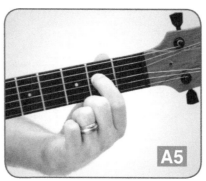

Figure 14

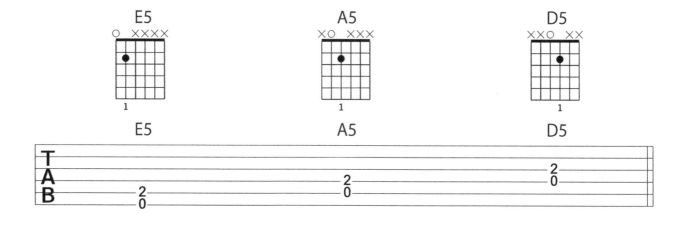

Figure 15a - *Whole notes*

Figure 15b - *Quarter notes*

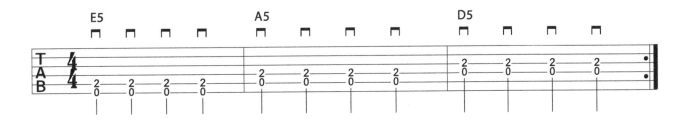

Figure 15c - *Eighth notes*

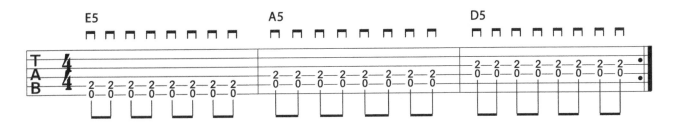

PRACTICE TIP!

Power Chord Strums

■ Make sure to sound the strings simultaneously, returning to the starting point after each strum.

LESSON 6

BLUES BASICS

Learning to play the blues serves as a solid foundation for many other genres, especially rock and jazz. Due to the nature of its inherent simplicity, the blues is a great starting point for any guitarist.

COMPING PATTERNS

LET'S ADD A NEW NOTE to the power chords you learned in Lesson 5 by pressing your ring finger on the fourth fret of the same string to create a 6th chord. Using only downstrokes, strum each chord twice, moving back and forth between the 2nd and 4th frets, maintaining an even tempo (**FIGURES 16A-C**). This type of pattern is known as *comping*, which is short for accompaniment.

Figure 16a

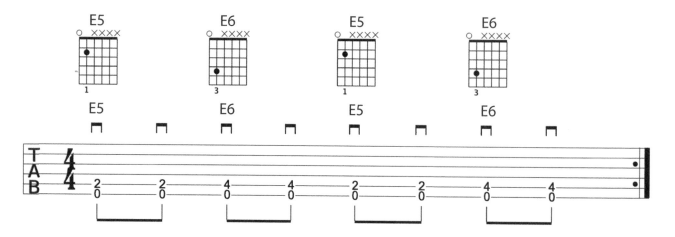

Figure 16b

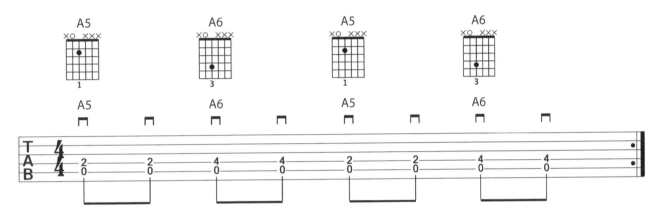

Figure 16c

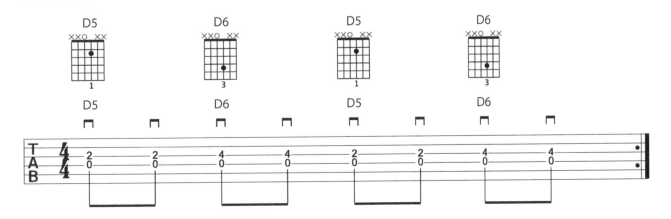

PLAYING A SHUFFLE

MOST BLUES SONGS are played with what is called a *shuffle feel* which has a lopsided sounding rhythm "DAH-duh-DAH-duh-DAH-duh-DAH-duh". First, start by playing a measure of eighth-note triplets (**FIGURE 17A**). In order to create a shuffle rhythm, play only the first and last notes of each triplet (**FIGURE 17B-C**). Shuffle rhythms are often written using straight eighth notes to keep things simple and can be called shuffle feel, triplet feel, etc. (**FIGURE 18**).

Figure 17a - *Triplet*

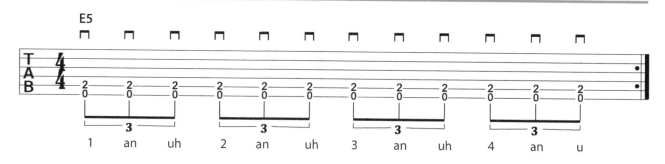

Figure 17b - *Shuffle*

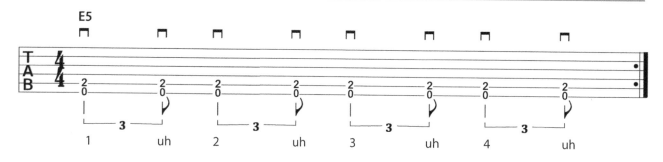

Figure 17c - *Comping pattern*

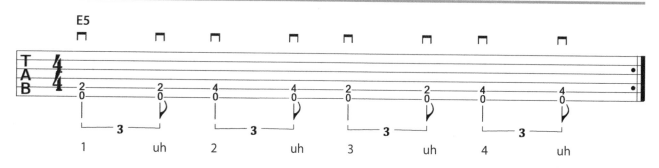

Figure 18

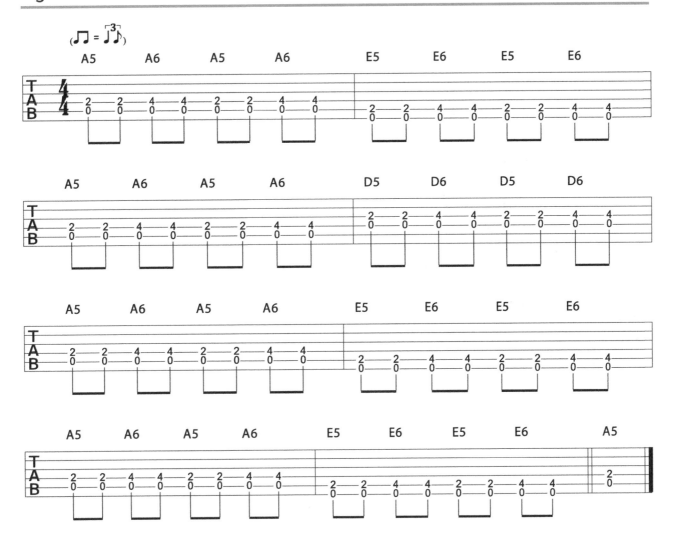

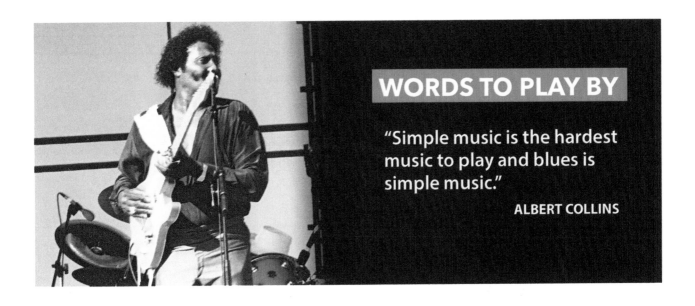

WORDS TO PLAY BY

"Simple music is the hardest music to play and blues is simple music."

ALBERT COLLINS

LESSON 7

PLAYING A RIFF

Similar to a melody, a riff is a short musical theme that is repeated throughout a piece of music. Many popular songs are often identified by the main riff which can be a simple single note pattern like "Satisfaction" by The Rolling Stones or "Day Tripper" by The Beatles.

SINGLE-NOTE RIFFS

RIFFS CAN BE HEARD in all types of music, whether it is rock, blues, or country. The riff in **FIGURE 19** may sound familiar as it has been used by countless artists such as The Beatles and Eric Clapton. **FIGURE 20** has its roots in country and can be heard in many Johnny Cash songs. Our last riff (**FIGURE 21**) is a typical Chicago blues style riff made famous by artists such as Muddy Waters and Freddie King.

Figure 19 - *Rock*

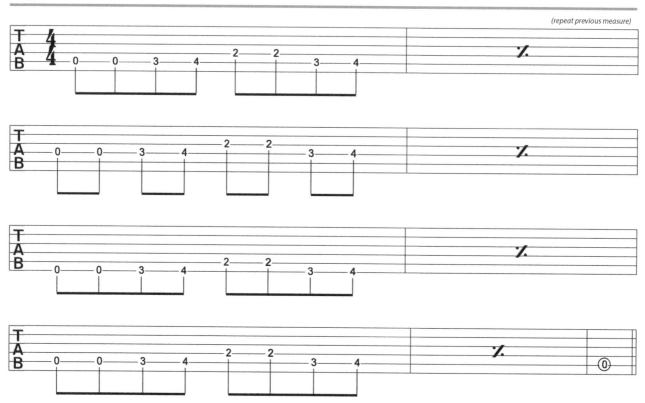

Figure 20 - *Country*

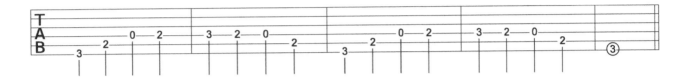

Figure 21 - *Blues*

PRACTICE TIP!

Learning Songs

When learning a new song, riff, or melody; take it in stages:

1. Identify the correct notes.

2. Work on the rhythm.

3. Slowly increase the tempo.

LESSON 8
POWER CHORD RIFFS

In this lesson, we will expand on the power chord shapes that you learned earlier through the use of three-note power chords. You'll also learn how to incorporate these new power chords with single-note riffs.

THREE-NOTE POWER CHORDS

BY ADDING ANOTHER NOTE to the power chords you can create a much fuller sound (**FIGURE 22**). The new note that has been added is the same as the root note but at a higher pitch and is called the *octave*. For the E5 and A5 chords, lay your index finger across the fretted strings on the second fret.

Figure 22

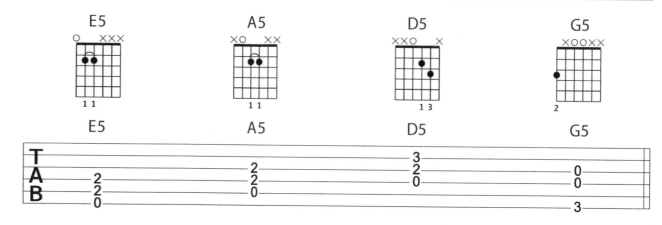

READING RESTS AND TIES

IN MUSIC, a *rest* is the absence of sound or when a note is silent. Just like the rhythms you have been playing, each rest gets a specific beat value (**FIGURE 23**). To effectively play a rest on the guitar, release the pressure of the fretting-hand while laying the fingers across the strings to mute the sound (**FIGURE 24**). *Tied* notes, on the other hand, link two notes together where the first note or chord is plucked and held for the duration of both notes (**FIGURE 25**). So far as riffs are concerned, rests and ties can make a sequence more interesting by breaking things up a little bit.

Figure 23 - *Rests*

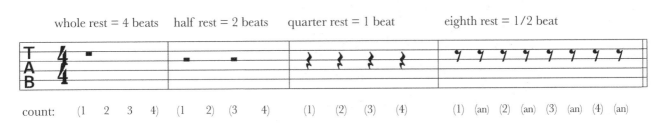

Figure 24

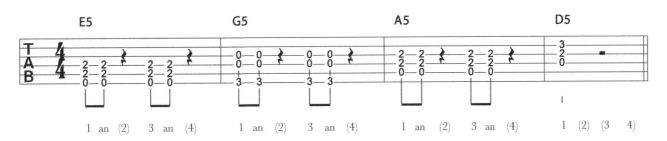

Figure 25 - *Ties*

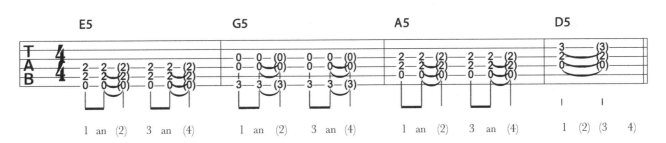

POWER CHORDS AND SINGLE-NOTES

AN OFTEN USED TECHNIQUE is to combine power chords with single notes to create a melodic chordal riff (**FIGURES 26-27**).

Figure 26

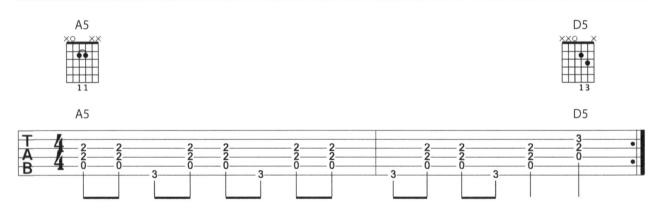

Figure 27

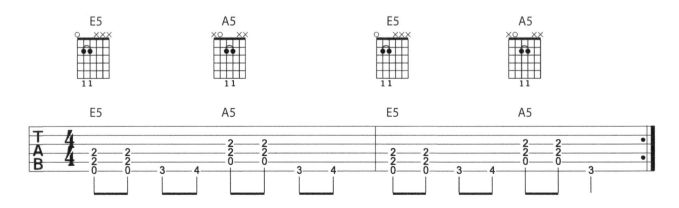

STRING BENDING

WHEN PLAYING SINGLE-NOTE RIFFS, a commonly used technique is *string bending*. The idea is to pull or push the string (depending on which string) across the fretboard to get the desired pitch. **FIGURE 28** incorporates a half step bend where the string is pulled down until it matches the pitch of the next fret up (4th fret in this case).

Figure 28

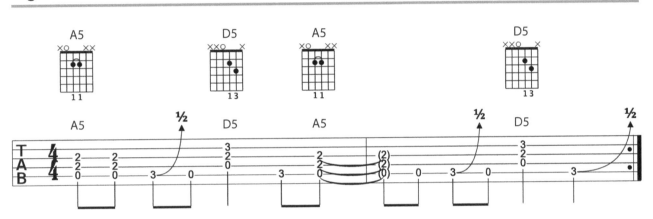

PRACTICE TIP!

String Bending

■ To properly execute a string bend on the lower strings, place your finger on the 5th string and pull it downward. A good practice technique is to sound the desired note first by fretting it and then bend the string until it matches the fretted note's pitch.

PART TWO

CHORDS & RHYTHM

LESSON 9

OPEN CHORDS

Open chords (sometimes referred to as "cowboy chords") are chords that are played in the open-position, meaning they require at least one open string. Widely used in all types of guitar music, mastering the open chords is essential for anyone wanting to play the guitar.

OPEN-POSITION MAJOR CHORDS

WHILE THE E MAJOR requires you to strum all six strings, the A major begins on the 5th string and can be fretted placing the index, middle, and ring fingers at a slight angle to fit into the 2nd fret. Use the same fingers to play the D major, starting the strum on the 4th string.

Figure 29

E	A	D
2 3 1	1 2 3	1 3 2

E
```
0
0
1
2
2
0
```

A
```
0
2
2
2
0
```

D
```
2
3
2
0
```

SIMILAR TO THE PREVIOUS THREE CHORDS, the G major uses the same fingers (1,2,3) spread across the fretboard and strummed with all six strings. For the C major, start on the A string, making sure the G and E strings ring out. The F chord is technically not an open chord, as it does not include any open strings. That being said, it is commonly grouped with the open chords. Perhaps the most difficult of all the chords, the F chord includes the first three fingers as well as the pinky.

Figure 30

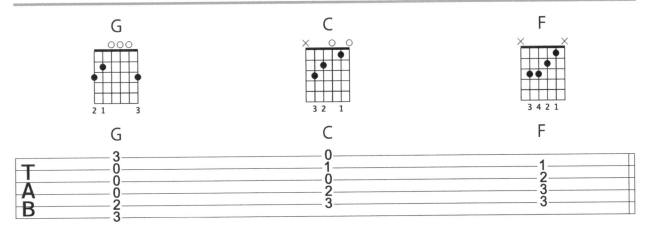

PRACTICE TIP!

Fretting a chord

To make your chords sound better, make sure you're pressing down hard enough, maintaining even pressure on the strings. Remember to keep your fingers curled, playing on the tips and not the pads.

OPEN-POSITION MINOR CHORDS

As was mentioned in Lesson 2, minor chords have a sadder, moodier sound than the major chords. In **FIGURE 31**, notice that the highest fret note for the E, A, D chords has been lowered by one fret changing them to minor chords. This note is called the third, as it is the 3rd scale degree of the major scale. A major chord is built from the 1st, 3rd, and 5th scales degrees, and when the 3rd scale degree is lowered one fret down, it becomes a minor chord (see page 111 *Chord Construction*).

Figure 31

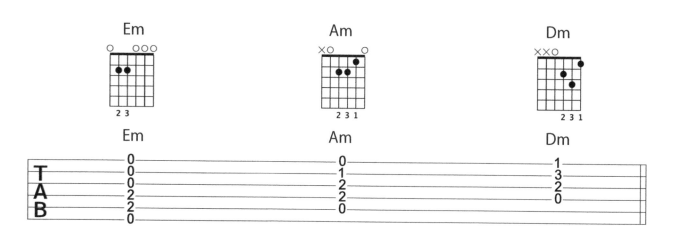

WORDS TO PLAY BY

"Sometimes you want to give up the guitar, you'll hate the guitar. But if you stick with it, you're gonna be rewarded."

JIMI HENDRIX

LESSON 10
CHORD SWITCHING

Once you are able to play the open chord shapes that you learned in the last lesson, the next step is to practice switching between the chords. In this lesson you'll learn some common chord changes used in many popular songs.

COMMON CHORD CHANGES

MANY SONGS TYPICALLY have a pattern of short (two or three) combinations of chord changes. It is important to practice these chord combinations on a daily basis so that the changes become automatic and effortless. The hash marks in each measure represent one beat. Start out by strumming and holding the chord for the entire measure, striving for a clear tone and even chord change before working up to strumming on each beat.

Figure 32

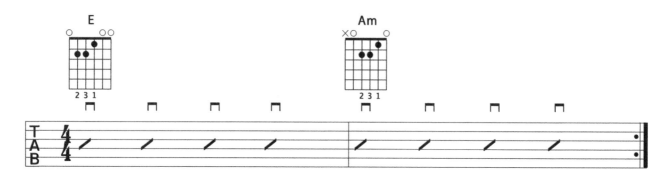

Figure 33

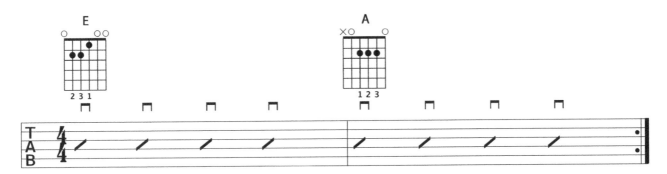

Figure 34

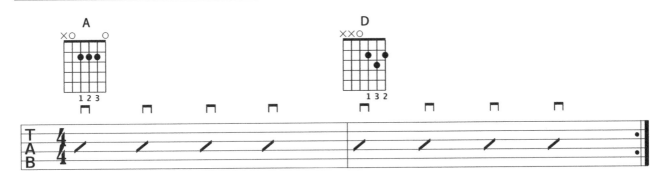

PRACTICE TIP!

The 'Pivot' method

For some chord changes, you can use one finger to function as a pivot for your other fingers. When switching from A to D, for example, keep your ring finger on the second string, shifting it up to the third fret to form the D chord.

Figure 35

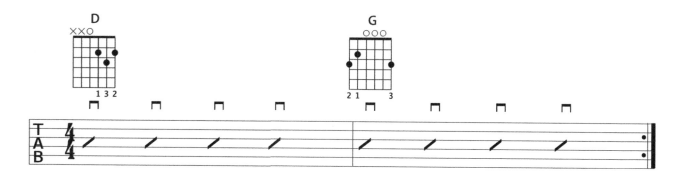

Figure 36

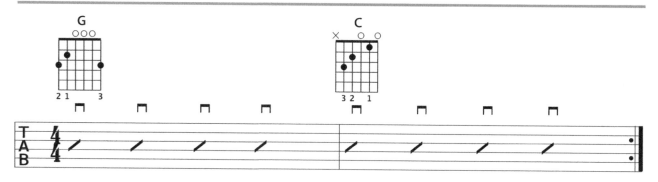

Figure 37

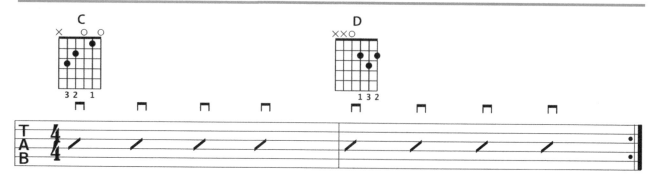

Figure 38

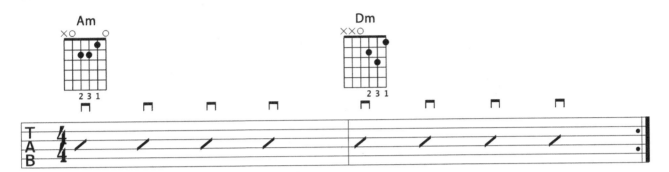

Figure 39

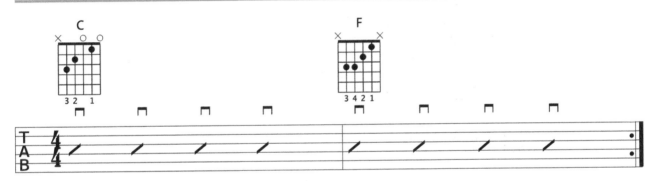

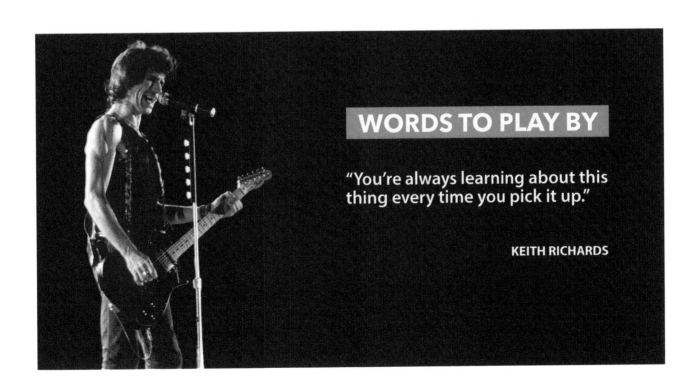

WORDS TO PLAY BY

"You're always learning about this thing every time you pick it up."

KEITH RICHARDS

LESSON 11
CHORD PROGRESSIONS

Now that you've got a handle on the chord changes, the next step is to put them into a repeated pattern called a chord progression. In this lesson you'll learn some common chord progressions favored by many musicians.

MAJOR CHORD PROGRESSIONS

CHORD PROGRESSIONS USUALLY contain a tonal center called a *key* that gives them a defined sound. The first chord is usually what defines the tonal center and the name of the key. For example, if the first chord is A major then the chord progression will be in the key of A major. **FIGURES 40-45** are some common major chord progressions used in thousands of songs. Just as you did with the chord changes in Lesson 10, practice each of these daily to become familiar with the patterns.

Figure 40 - *Key of A*

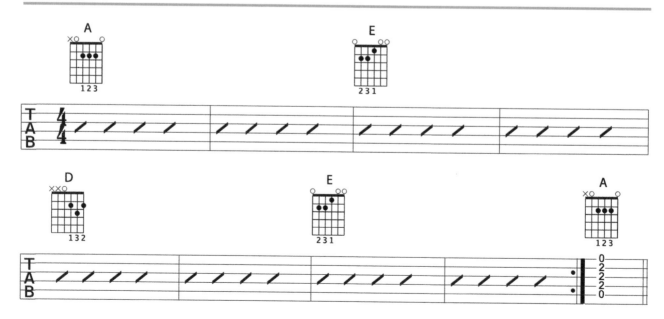

Figure 41 - *Key of D*

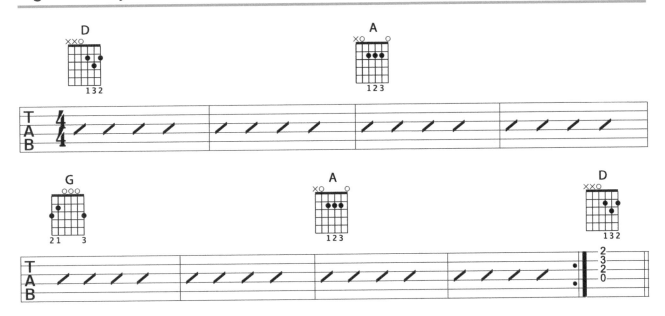

Figure 42 - *Key of E*

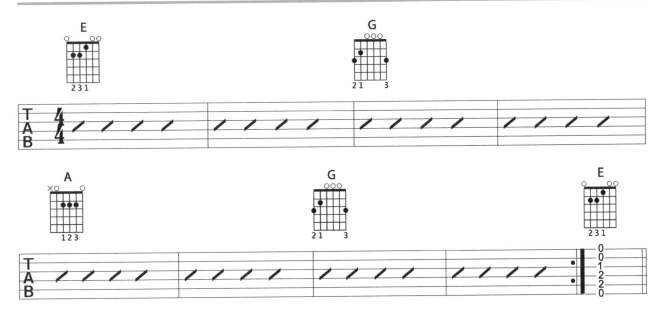

Figure 43 - *Key of G*

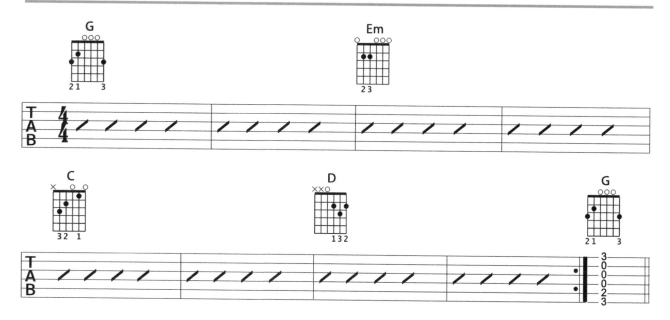

Figure 44 - *Key of C*

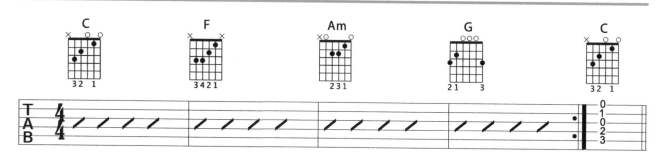

▶ TRACK LIST	Popular Open Chord Songs
"Knockin' On Heaven's Door" (G-D-Am-C)	Bob Dylan
"Love Me Do" (G-C-D)	The Beatles
"Three Little Birds" (A-D-E)	Bob Marley
"Free Fallin'" (D-G-A)	Tom Petty
"Brown Eyed Girl" (G-C-D-Em)	Van Morrison
"La Bamba" (C-F-G)	Ritchie Valens

MINOR CHORD PROGRESSIONS

YOU MAY HAVE NOTICED that the major chord progressions have a happy sound to them. Though not always the case, many sad or moodier songs are written in a minor key such as "Wish You Were Here" by Pink Floyd and "Dream On" by Aerosmith.

Figure 45 - *Key of Em*

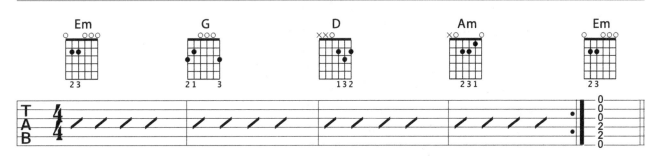

Figure 46 - *Key of Am*

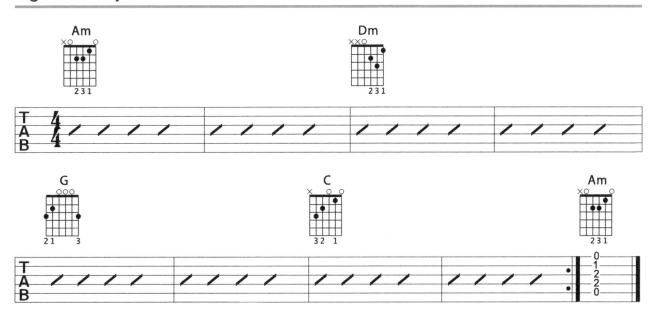

LESSON 12
STRUM PATTERNS

Most guitar based songs are written with a preset rhythmic pattern called a strum pattern. In this lesson, you'll learn several strum patterns that have been used in thousands of songs and can be applied to all of the chord progressions that you have learned so far.

GAINING RHYTHMIC CONTROL

LET'S START WITH A simple two chord pattern using only eighth notes (**FIGURE 47**). It is important to learn to strum with a steady, even tempo, tapping your foot as you play. Keep your strumming hand relaxed as this will help you create a nice, smooth rhythm.

Figure 47

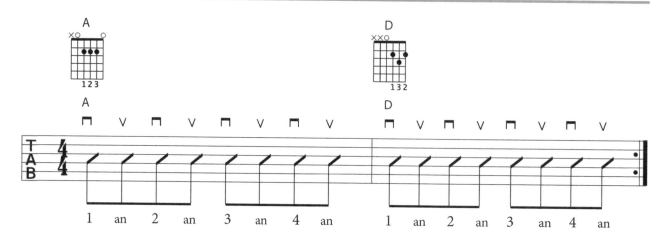

FOR THE NEXT EXAMPLES, we'll add in some quarter notes (**FIGURES 48-49**). It's helpful to practice the patterns by muting the strings with your fretting hand so that you can isolate the rhythm pattern. You can also practice a new rhythm pattern with only one chord and then gradually add the others.

Figure 48

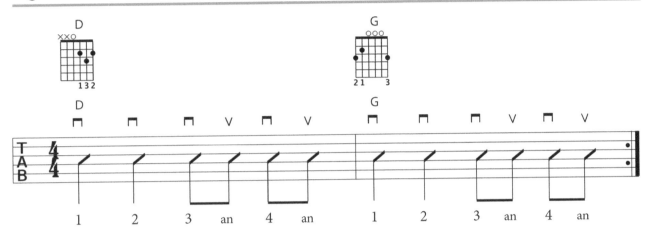

Figure 49

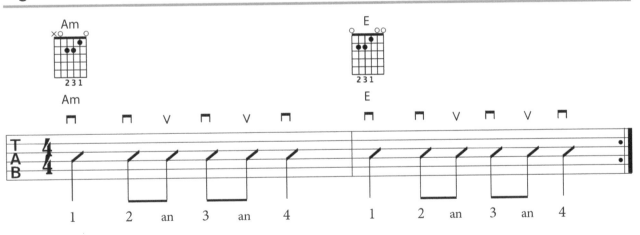

PRACTICE TIP!

Use a metronome

Start with a very slow tempo (65bpm) accenting the downbeats. This will help you maintain a clean and even sound rather than just a flurry of notes.

THE SYNCOPATED STRUM

To make a strum pattern more interesting, many guitarists will play a *syncopated* pattern, where the strums are played in unexpected places. To play the syncopated pattern in **FIGURE 50**, fake the strum over the third beat so you are set up for the upstroke on the next eighth note.

Figure 50

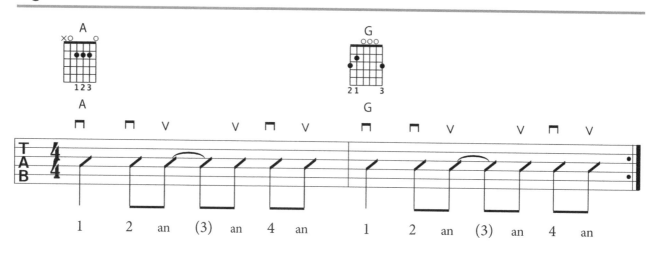

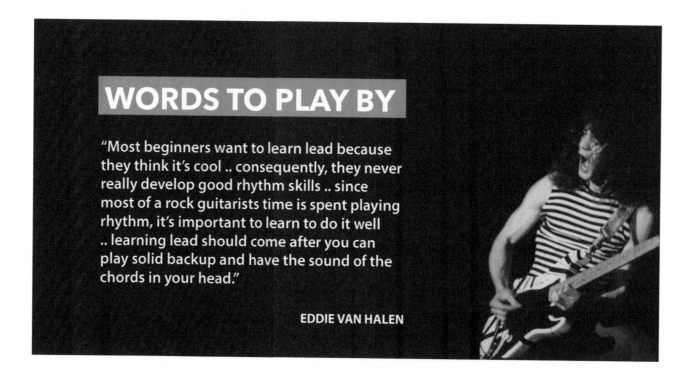

WORDS TO PLAY BY

"Most beginners want to learn lead because they think it's cool .. consequently, they never really develop good rhythm skills .. since most of a rock guitarists time is spent playing rhythm, it's important to learn to do it well .. learning lead should come after you can play solid backup and have the sound of the chords in your head."

EDDIE VAN HALEN

SIXTEENTH NOTE STRUMS

IF YOU DIVIDE an eighth note in half you get a *sixteenth note*, which is a 1/4 of a beat. Count: "ONE-e-an-uh-TWO-e-an-uh-THREE-e-an-uh-FOUR-e-an-uh"

Figure 51

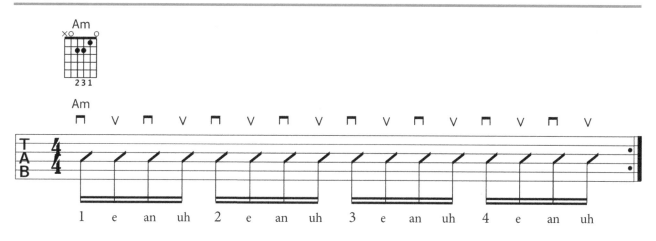

Figure 52

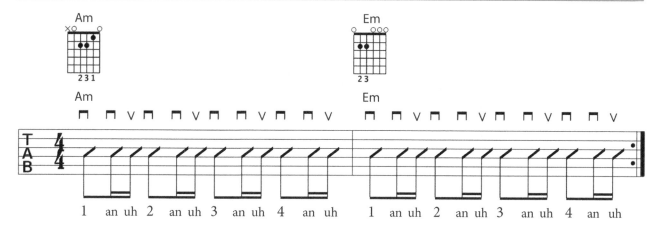

Figure 53

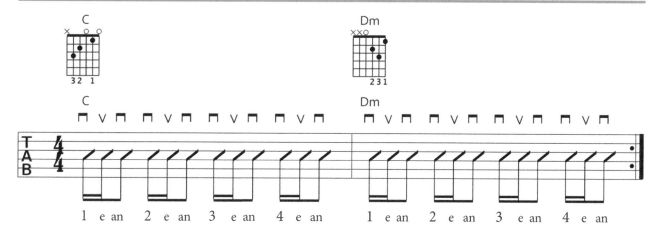

LESSON 13
SEVENTH CHORDS

Let's expand your chord vocabulary and add in some seventh chords, also known as dominant seventh chords. Often used in blues and jazz music, seventh chords can add more texture and color to a simple chord progression.

DOMINANT SEVENTH CHORDS

DOMINANT SEVENTH CHORDS ARE BUILT by combining the first, third, fifth and flatted seventh degrees of the major scale (see page 111 *Chord Construction*). Even though they have a fancy name, dominant seventh chords (**FIGURE 54**) or simply *7th chords* are relatively easy to play.

Figure 54

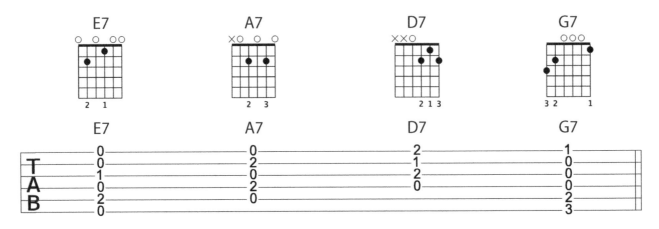

WHILE MAJOR CHORDS are stable or *consonant* sounding, the seventh chord has an unstable or *dissonant* sound. Notice how the seventh chords in **FIGURES 55-56** want to "move" to the next chord, giving the progression a richer, harmonic quality.

Figure 55

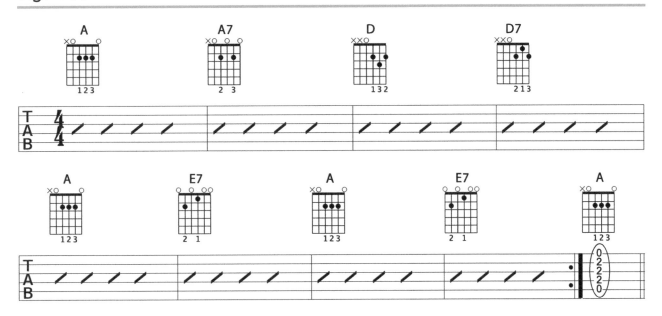

Figure 56

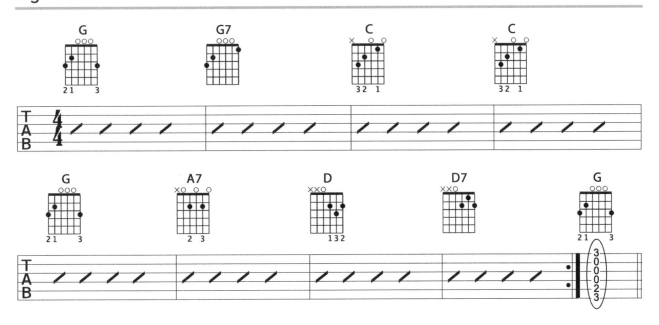

THE 12 BAR BLUES PROGRESSION

THE 12 BAR BLUES PROGRESSION is simply a chord progression that lasts for twelve measures. Though rooted primarily in blues music, the 12 bar blues is perhaps the most prominent chord progression in popular music. Famous 12 bar songs include "Rock Around the Clock," "Blue Suede Shoes," and "Johnny B. Goode." A commonly used technique is playing the entire progression with only seventh chords (**FIGURE 57**).

Figure 57 - *Shuffle feel*

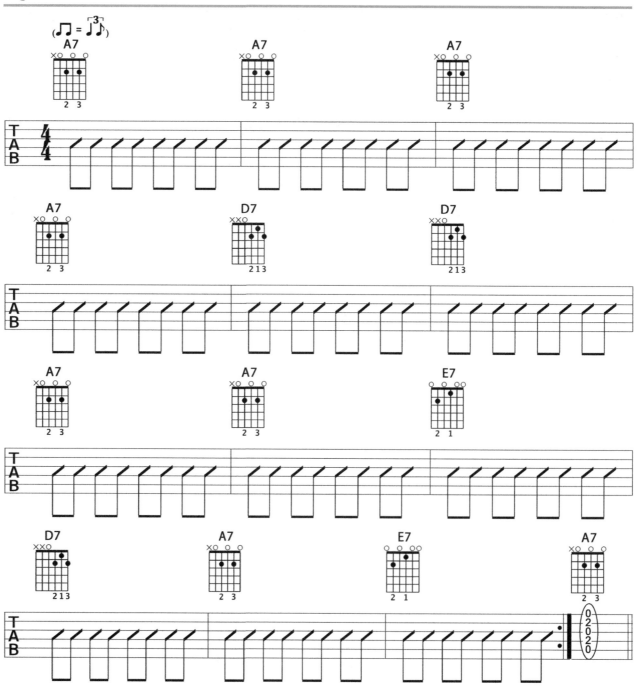

WORDS TO PLAY BY

"Let me explain something about guitar playing. Everyone's got their own character, and that's the thing that's amazed me about guitar playing since the day I first picked it up. Everyone's approach to what can come out of six strings is different from another person, but it's all valid."

JIMMY PAGE

LESSON 14
CHORDAL TECHNIQUES

In the last two lessons, the focus has been on the use of common chords and strumming patterns. Now let's expand on these concepts through the use of different picking patterns and chordal techniques.

PICKING PATTERNS

A USEFUL METHOD when playing an arpeggio is to use downstrokes when the sequence travels towards the higher (thinner) strings and upstrokes when the sequence travels towards the lower (thicker) strings. This technique is also known as *economy picking* (**FIGURES 58-59**).

Figure 58

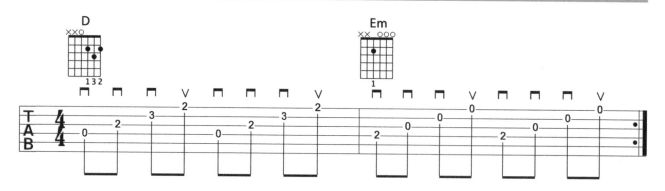

Figure 59

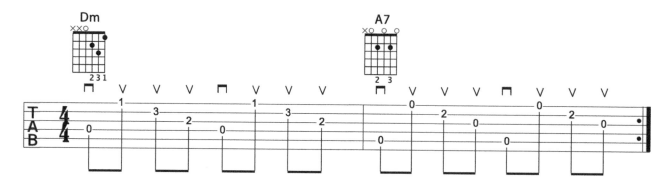

ARPEGGIATED PATTERNS CAN BE CREATED several different ways depending on the chord shape. **FIGURE 60** is an example of starting on the root note (4th string for D and 5th string for A) and then playing a mixed pattern on the top three strings (1st, 2nd, and 3rd). **FIGURE 61** takes this idea a step further by using a full chord strum followed by a syncopated picking pattern.

Figure 60

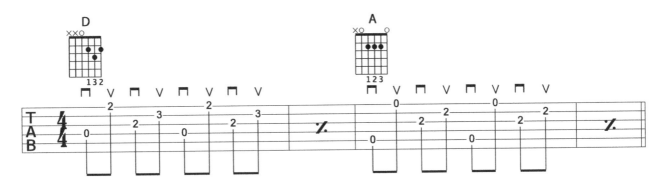

Figure 61

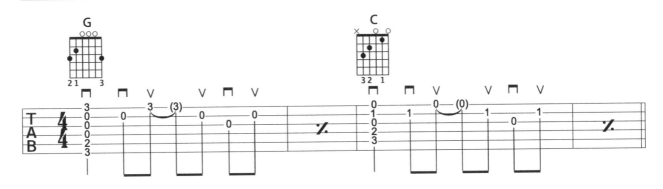

▶ TRACK LIST	Essential Arpeggio Riffs
"House of the Rising Sun"	The Animals
"Good Riddance (Time of Your Life)"	Green Day
"Here Comes the Sun"	The Beatles
"Ain't Talkin' Bout Love"	Van Halen
"What It's Like"	Everlast
"Sweet Home Alabama"	Lynyrd Skynyrd

THE BASS STRUM

BUILDING ON THE STRUM PATTERNS you learned in Lesson 12, the *bass strum* is a technique that incorporates a single bass note and chord strum. To emphasis the bass notes, only the upper strings of the chord are strummed. **FIGURE 62** is a bass strum pattern that uses the root note of the chord for the bass, while **FIGURE 63** includes both the root note and another note of the chord, creating what is termed *alternating bass*.

Figure 62

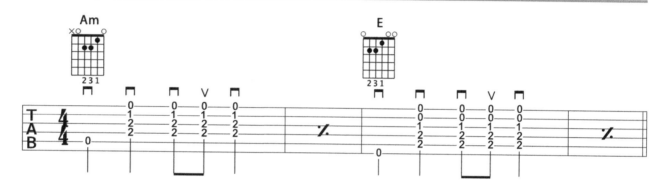

Figure 63

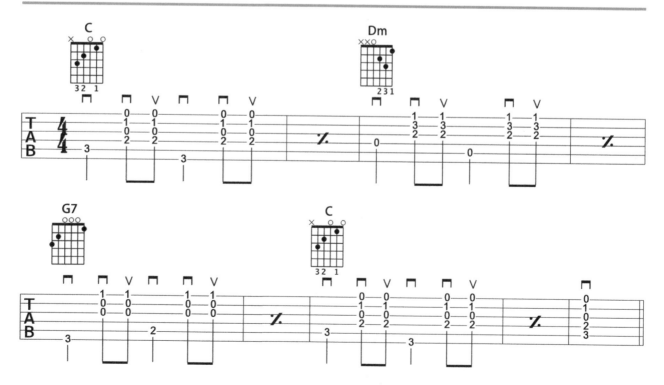

HAMMER-ONS AND PULL-OFFS

YOU CAN FURTHER ENHANCE your chords and make a chord progression more interesting through the use of *hammer-ons* and *pull-offs*. To execute a hammer-on, pluck a string and then sound another note higher up on the same string by "hammering" or tapping your finger down on the fretboard. A pull-off reverses this concept in that the string is plucked and the lower note is sounded by slightly "pulling" or tugging the string. Adding in some altered chords, **FIGURE 64** shows how hammer-ons and pull-offs are used to create a *walking bass line*.

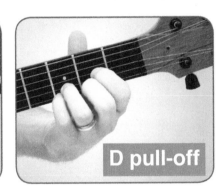

Figure 64

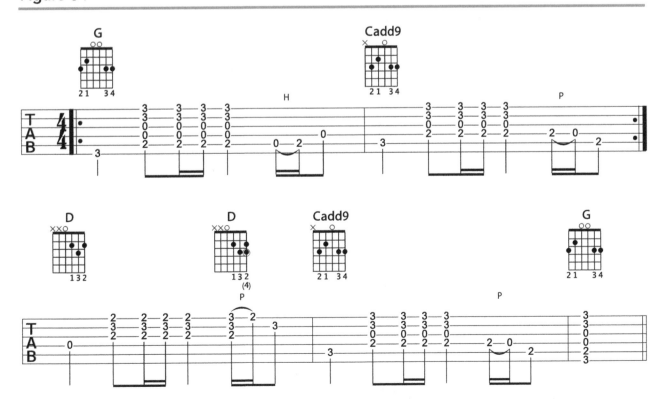

PART THREE

MOVING UP THE

FRETBOARD

LESSON 15
MOVEABLE CHORDS

Up until now, all of the chords have been played in the open-position. Starting with the power chords, you'll now learn how chords can be transformed to move up and down the fretboard.

SIXTH-STRING-ROOT POWER CHORDS

REMEMBER THAT A CHORD is defined by the root note so, for example, if the root note is E, then the chord is E, whether it is major, minor, power chord, etc. In the example below (**FIGURE 65**), notice how the root note on the 6th string changes as does the chord name.

Figure 65

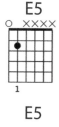
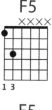

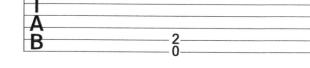

A GOOD WAY to get more familiar with the moveable power chord shape is to practice playing it chromatically up and down the fretboard. Below is a graph showing the order of notes on the 6th string (**FIGURE 66A**). When you ascend up the fretboard, the pattern is the letter followed by the same letter with a sharp (i.e., A to A♯). The same rule applies when you descend, except that the sharps are changed to flats (A to A♭). The only exception to this rule is B to C and E to F. For now, focus only on the ascending order, calling out each chord name as you play it (**FIGURE 66B**).

Figure 66a

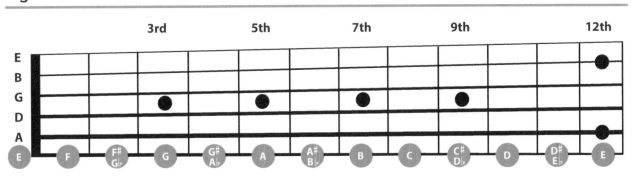

Figure 66b

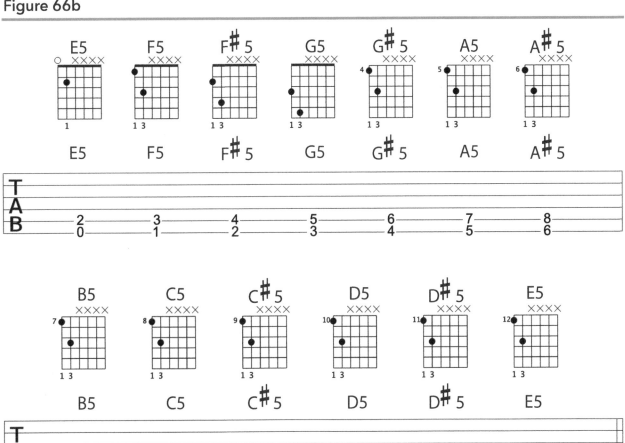

NOW THAT YOU'RE FAMILIAR with the chord shapes, let's practice some common chordal movements (**FIGURES 67-68**).

Figure 67

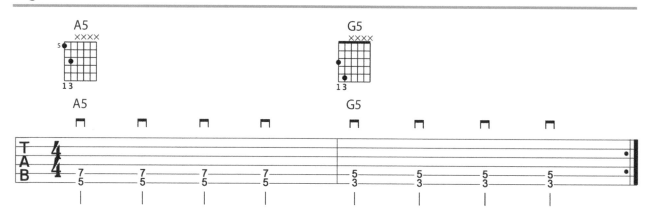

Figure 68

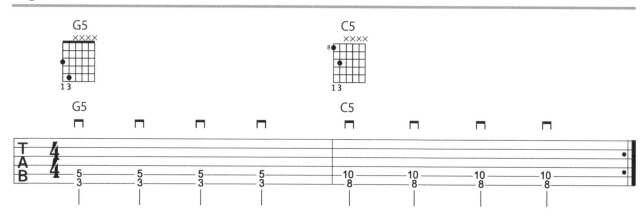

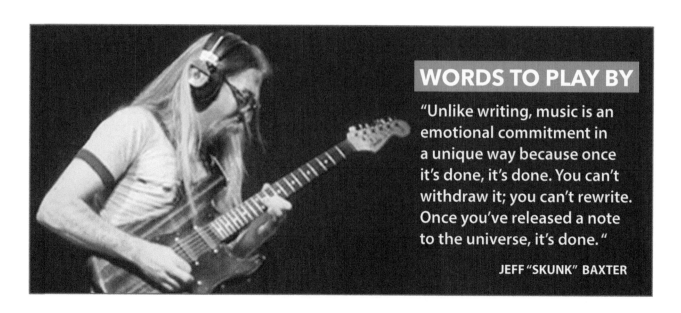

FIFTH-STRING-ROOT POWER CHORDS

Now that you have sixth-string root power chords down, you can shift to the next set of strings to play fifth-string root power chords. Even though the notes are different, the same principle applies in that the root note is the bottom string (**FIGURE 69**). To prevent the sixth string from accidentally ringing out, use the tip of the index finger to lightly mute the string.

Figure 69

JUST AS YOU DID previously, practice the fifth-string root power chords chromatically, reciting the chord names as you play (**FIGURES 70A-B**).

Figure 70a

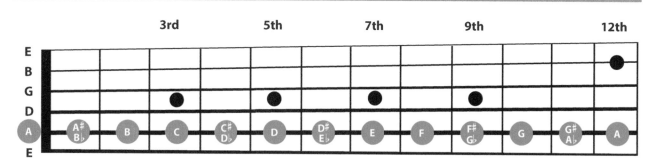

Figure 70b

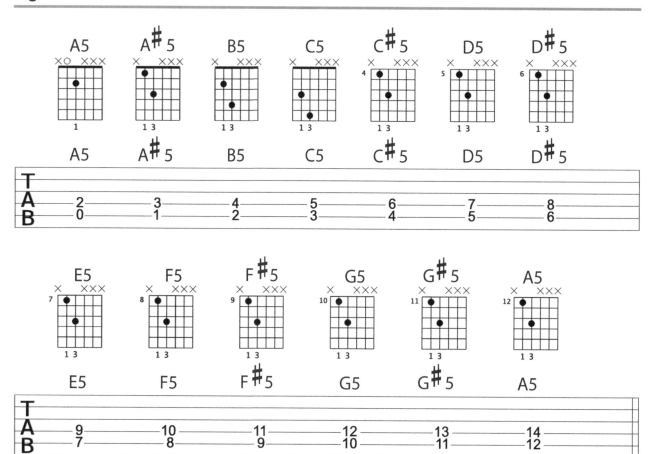

COMBINING SIXTH AND FIFTH-STRING ROOT POWER CHORDS

INSTEAD OF JUST MAKING wide jumps up and down the fretboard, you can combine both power chord shapes and stay within one area of the fretboard. **FIGURES 71-73** are a few examples that utilize this concept.

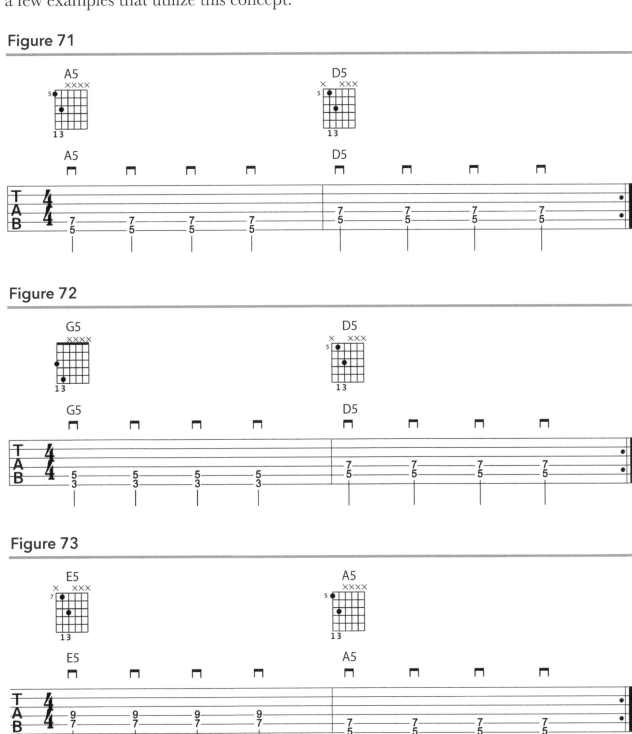

Figure 71

Figure 72

Figure 73

LESSON 16
RIFFING TECHNIQUES

Many power chord based riffs utilize various articulation techniques to achieve different sounds. In this lesson, we'll explore some common techniques that are in many power chord based riffs.

PALM MUTING

LET'S BEGIN with a popular technique called *palm muting.* Used primarily in rock, blues and metal, palm muting produces a strong, percussive sound when executed correctly. Take the knife edge of your hand and lay it gently across the strings closest to the bridge. Keeping your hand in the same position, strike the 6th, 5th, and 4th strings by pivoting with your wrist (**FIGURE 74**).

Figure 74

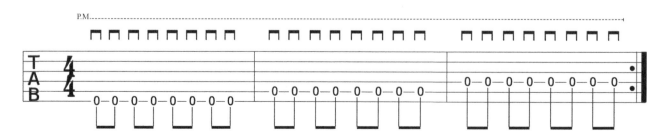

PEDAL TONES

A note that is repeatedly sounded while the notes around it change is referred to as a *pedal tone* or *pedal note*. Some classic examples of pedal tone riffs are "Whole Lotta Love" by Led Zeppelin and "Master of Puppets" by Metallica. In guitar music, the pedal tone will usually be one of the lower strings accented by a single-note, or chord, on the upper strings (**FIGURES 75-76**).

Figure 75

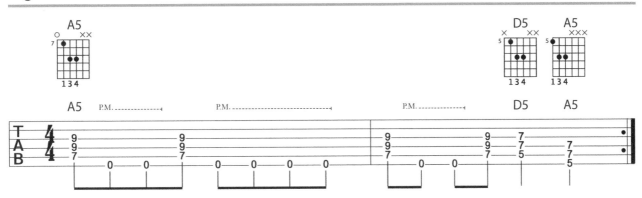

Figure 76

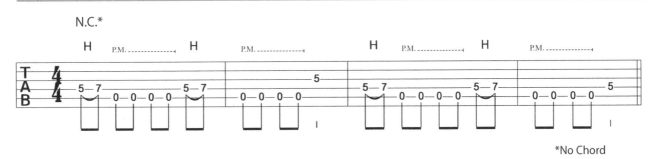

*No Chord

SLIDES

SLIDES ARE ANOTHER really cool effect that can breathe more life into a riff. The idea is that you move from one fret to the next by plucking the first note(s) and then slide to the next note(s) on the same string. There are two different types of slides: *legato slides* and *shift slides*. Legato slides are notated with a straight line and an arch linking the two notes together. To perform a legato slide, simply pluck the first note and slide to the next note with the same finger(s) (**FIGURE 77**). A shift slide is notated with only a straight line and is performed the same way, except that the second note(s) is plucked again after the slide (**FIGURE 78**).

Figure 77

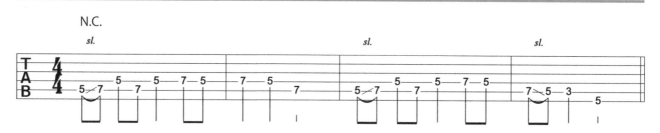

Figure 78

PRACTICE TIP!

Slides

■ Maintain constant finger pressure as you slide up or down the string. Be careful not to press too hard as it can lose its effect.

GALLOP RHYTHMS

WIDELY USED IN THE MORE heavier forms of rock music, the *gallop rhythm* gets its name from the fact that it is reminiscent of the sound of a galloping animal. The rhythm consists of an eighth, followed by two sixteenth notes that are played with a down-down-up picking motion. The pattern can be played using only a single repeated note (**FIGURE 79**) or used in conjunction with power chords (**FIGURE 80**).

Figure 79

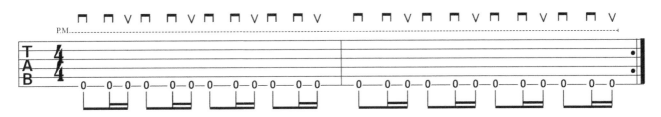

Figure 80

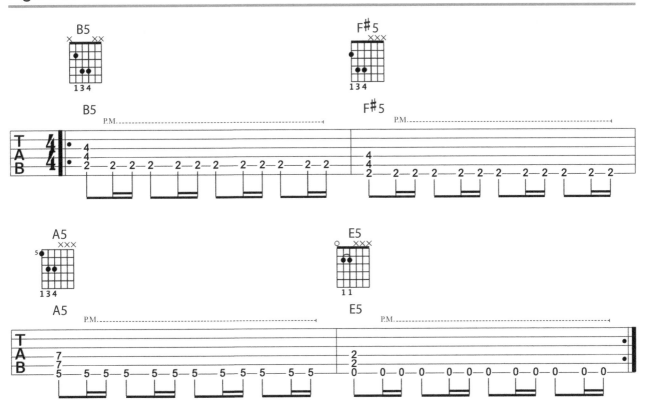

LESSON 17
ESSENTIAL BLUES RIFFS

So far we've covered a few basic blues patterns and rhythms that are commonly used in many types of music. In this lesson, we'll further explore some important riffs and techniques used in blues music.

TURNAROUNDS

MOST BLUES SONGS contain a musical technique called a *turnaround* which is a two bar melodic phrase that signifies the end of a section. In **FIGURE 81**, the turnaround begins on the second to last measure. **FIGURE 82** utilizes a single-note descending pattern used in conjunction with the 7th chords.

Figure 81 - *Shuffle Feel*

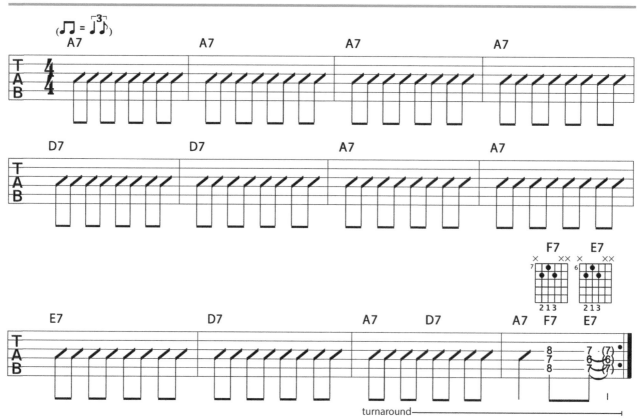

Figure 82

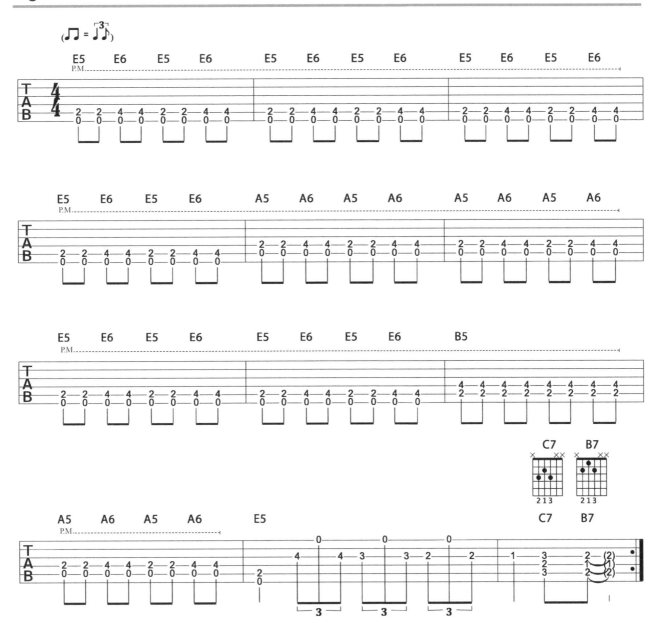

TRACK LIST	Essential Blues Songs	
"Hoochie Coochie Man"	Muddy Waters
"Dust My Broom"	Elmore James
"Sweet Home Chicago"	Robert Johnson
"Killing Floor"	Howlin' Wolf
"Red House"	Jimi Hendrix
"Pride and Joy"	Stevie Ray Vaughn

THE BLUES BOOGIE

ANOTHER COMMON BLUES TECHNIQUE is to play single-note patterns similar to what a bass player would play. **FIGURE 83** demonstrates this *blues boogie* style, adding an ascending turnaround pattern.

Figure 83

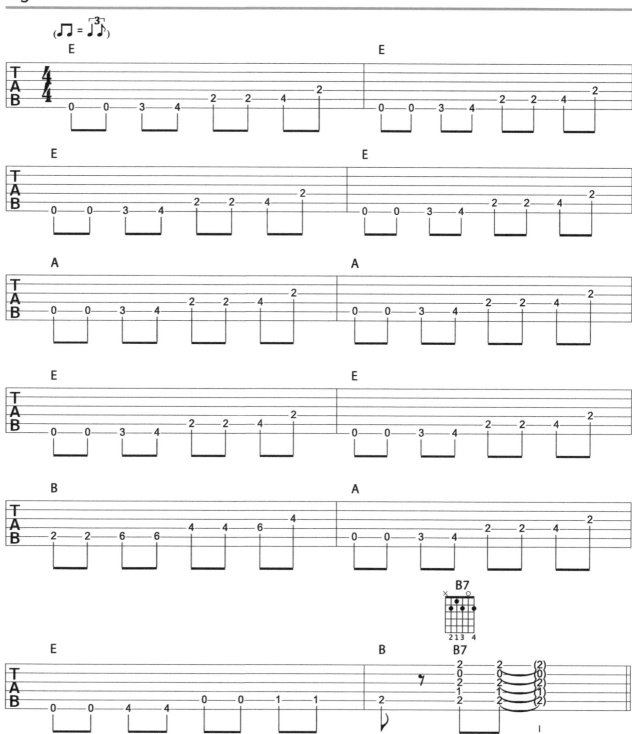

HOW TO PLAY A MOVEABLE BLUES PROGRESSION

THE BLUES PATTERNS that we have looked at so far have all been in the open position. Knowing how to play in multiple keys is handy, especially when vocals are involved. **FIGURE 84** shows how the power chord shapes can be changed into a comping pattern using your pinky to create the necessary chord extension.

 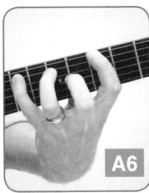  

Figure 84

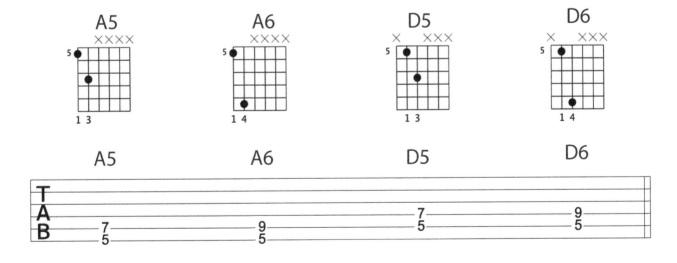

NOW LET'S TAKE the moveable chord extensions and apply them to a 12 bar blues progression (**FIGURE 85**). This progression has a slightly different arrangement than the previous progressions we've played thus far. Watch out for the quick change to the D5-D6 in the second measure, as well as the turnaround pattern.

Figure 85

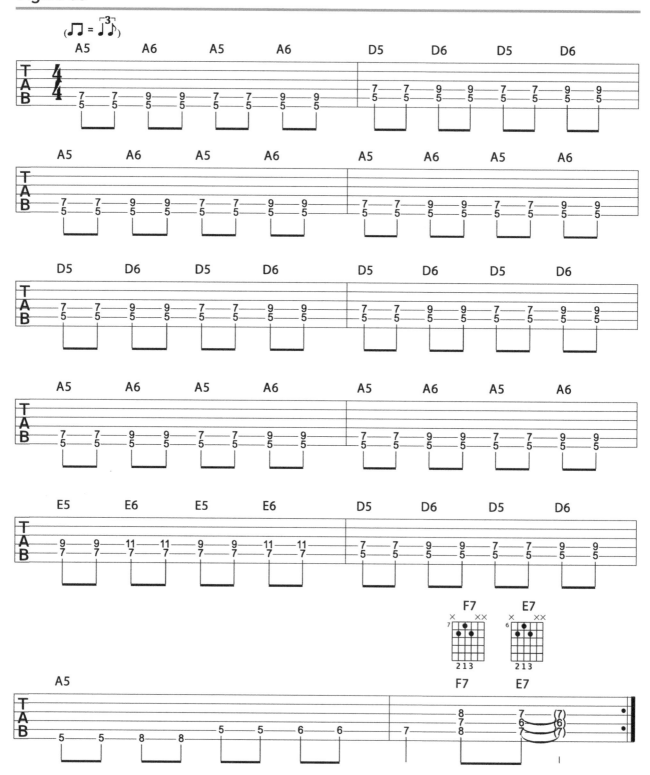

WORDS TO PLAY BY

"The beautiful thing about learning is nobody can take it away from you."

B.B. KING

LESSON 18

BARRE CHORDS

Just like the power chords, barre chords are moveable chord shapes but require the index finger to fret all of the strings on one fret. In this lesson we will take a look at playing the full major, minor, and seventh barre chord shapes.

SIXTH-STRING-ROOT MAJOR AND MINOR BARRE CHORDS

A BARRE CHORD is essentially a moveable open chord shape with a modified fingering. In **FIGURE 86** notice how the E major chord is shifted up one fret using a "3 4 2" fingering. The index finger replaces the nut by laying across all six strings. Removing the middle finger creates the minor barre chord shape.

Figure 86

E
2 3 1

F
1 3 4 2 1 1

Em
2 3

Fm
1 3 4 1 1 1

E

```
T  --0------------
A  --0------------
   --1------------
   --2------------
   --2------------
B  --0------------
```

F

```
--1------------
--1------------
--2------------
--3------------
--3------------
--1------------
```

Em

```
--0------------
--0------------
--0------------
--2------------
--2------------
--0------------
```

Fm

```
--1------------
--1------------
--1------------
--3------------
--3------------
--1------------
```

Figure 87

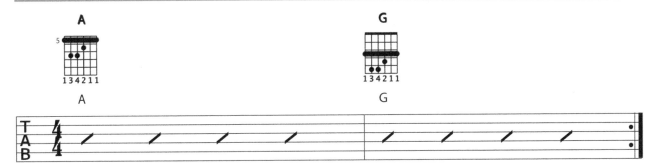

Figure 88

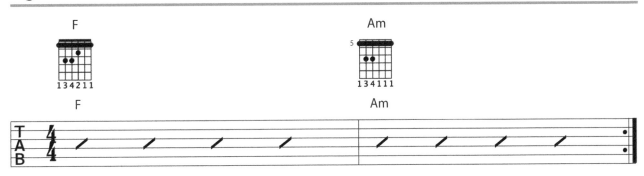

PRACTICE TIP!

Fretting a barre chord

■ Use gravity to aid in playing barre chords by allowing the weight of the elbow to fall down pulling the forearm back. This allows you to execute the barre chord without having to press as hard and fatiguing the left hand.

FIFTH-STRING-ROOT MAJOR AND MINOR BARRE CHORDS

ONE OF THE MOST CHALLENGING barre chords to play is the 5th string root major shape. Depending on where you are on the fretboard, you can use two different types of fingerings. In the lower positions where the frets are wider, you can employ the 2nd, 3rd and 4th fingers. As you move higher up the neck, where the frets are narrower, many guitarists (myself included) barre the strings with their 3rd finger. The only drawback is that it's nearly impossible to play it without muting the high E string. There is no rule that says you have to sound all of the strings of a chord, and in this case, it can actually sound better! Compared to the major shape, the 5th string root minor should seem relatively easy. **FIGURES 90-92** are a few examples of how all of the barre chord shapes can be played together.

Figure 89

Figure 90

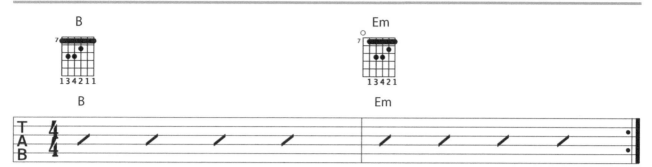

Figure 91

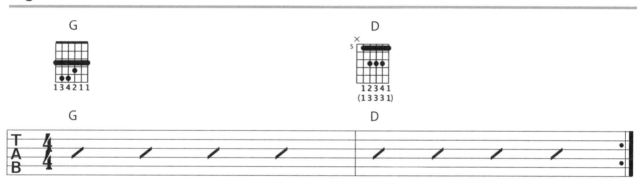

Figure 92

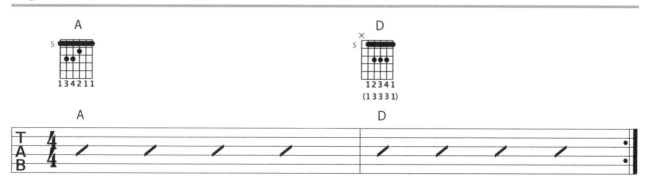

SIXTH AND FIFTH-STRING-ROOT BARRED SEVENTH CHORDS

KNOWING THE MOVEABLE 7th chord shapes is important as they are commonly found in many of your favorite rock, blues, country, jazz and reggae songs. The chord shapes work the same way as the major and minor chords with a modified fingering that may, in fact, be a little easier than some of the previous shapes.

  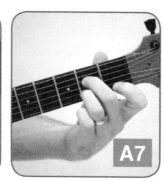 

Figure 93

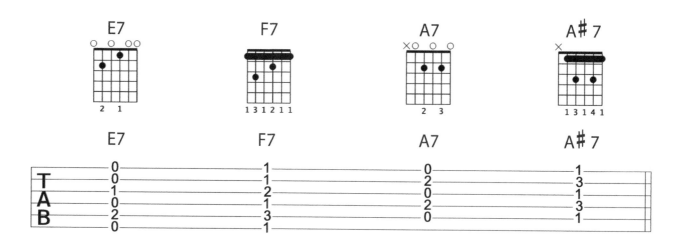

Figure 94

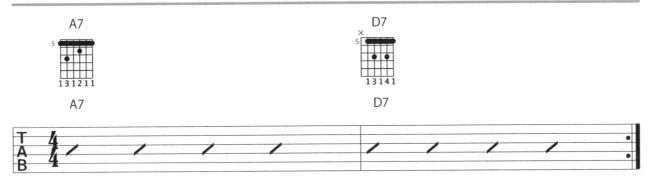

Figure 95

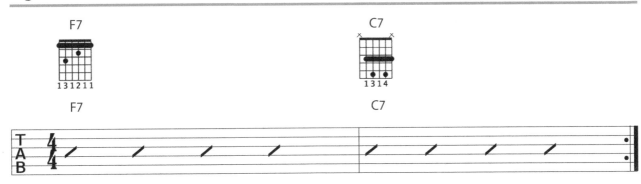

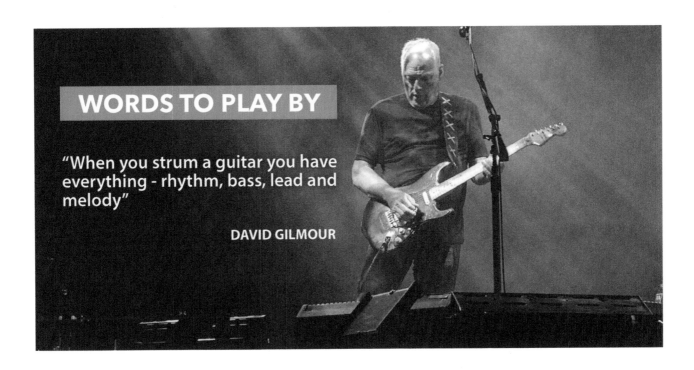

WORDS TO PLAY BY

"When you strum a guitar you have everything - rhythm, bass, lead and melody"

DAVID GILMOUR

LESSON 19

CHORD FAMILIES

So far, you have learned to play many different types of chord progressions without knowing why certain chords are grouped together. In this lesson you'll learn how chord families work and the most common chord progressions in popular music.

DIATONIC CHORDS

THINK OF DIATONIC CHORDS as a family of chords that are part of the same gene pool. Many, if not most, of the songs you hear use diatonic chords, meaning that they all share the same notes. These notes are part of the major scale which is made up of seven different notes. A *key* is simply the notes from the major scale that can be played in any order. For example, the notes in the key of C major are C-D-E-F-G-A-B; in the key of G, the notes are G-A-B-C-D-E-F♯, etc. These notes can be turned into chords by stacking every other note on top of each other. Major, minor, and diminished chords have only three notes, so for the C chord you have the notes: C-E-G; or for the Am chord: A-C-E etc. This creates a chord pattern labeled with Roman numerals that is the same for every key (**FIGURE 96**).

Figure 96 - *Diatonic chords in C major*

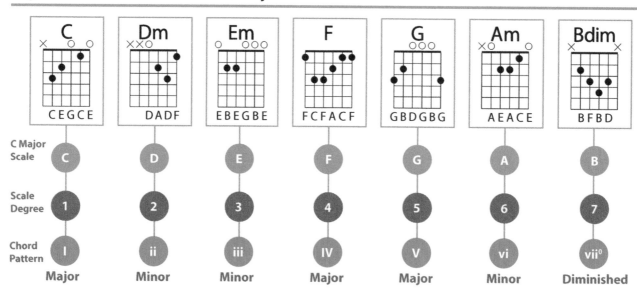

POPULAR CHORD PROGRESSIONS

WHILE THERE IS AN ENDLESS number of chord progressions that you can play, certain ones have been used over and over again. The I-IV-V progression is perhaps the most widely used in popular music and forms the basic structure of nearly every blues song. Using slight variations, the chord pattern can be used to play many classic songs such as "Love Me Do" by The Beatles, "Brown Eyed Girl" by Van Morrison, or "La Bamba" by Ritchie Valens. **FIGURE 97** shows the I-IV-V pattern in the key of C. For the next example in **FIGURE 98**, the chord pattern has been transposed to the key of G, which means that while the notes have changed, the quality of the chords remains the same. Using the key chart on page 110, practice playing the I-IV-V pattern in each key.

Figure 97 - *I-IV-V in C*

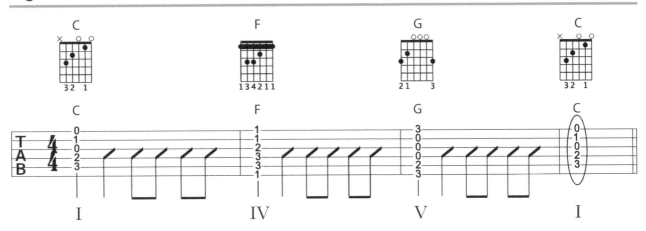

Figure 98 - *I-IV-V in G*

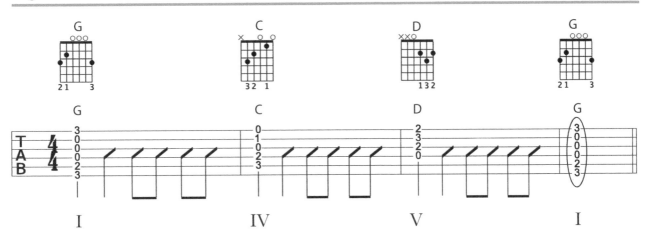

As was mentioned earlier, diatonic chord progressions can be played in various ways. In **FIGURE 99**, the I chord moves to the V chord instead of the IV. Another common practice is to make the V a dominant seventh chord (**FIGURE 100**). As dominant means "powerful" or "pushy," listen to how the V^7 wants to push back to the I chord. Expanding on the I-IV-V progression, many songs will also add in a minor chord. Sometimes called the "50's Progression," the I-vi-IV-V pattern (**FIGURE 101**) was used in many doo wop songs of the 1950's. It can also be heard in many hit songs such as "Stand By Me" by Ben E. King and "Every Breathe You Take" by The Police. Changing the order around gives you the I-V-vi-IV (**FIGURE 102**), which is famously referred to as the "Pop Progression" because it is perhaps the most often used chord progression in popular music. Use of this particular chord pattern can be heard in a wide variety of genres from "Take Me Home, Country Roads" by John Denver to "Under the Bridge" by the Red Hot Chili Peppers.

Figure 99 - *I-V-IV Progression in A*

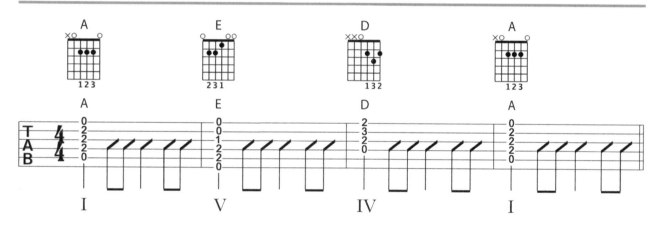

Figure 100 - *I-IV-V⁷ Progression in E*

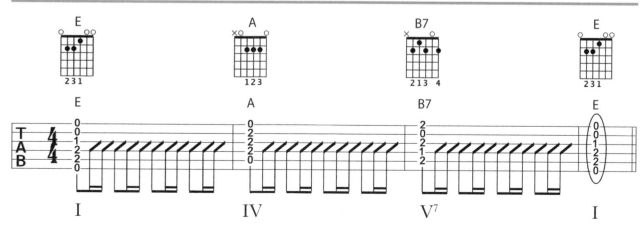

Figure 101 - *I-vi-IV-V Progression in D*

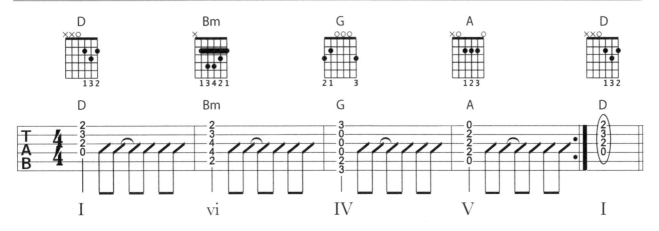

Figure 102 - *I-V-vi-IV Progression in F*

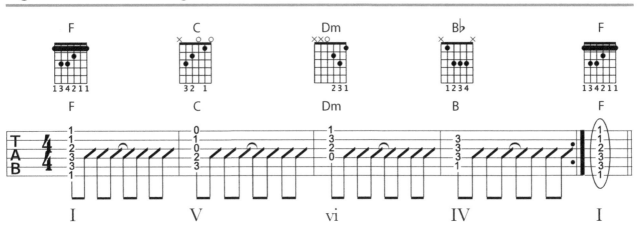

▶ TRACK LIST	Popular Chord Progressions
I-IV-V	"Twist and Shout" (The Beatles) / "Lay Down Sally" (Eric Clapton)
I-IV-V^7	"Folsom Prison" (Johnny Cash)
I-vi-IV-V	"Chain Gang" (Sam Cooke) / "No Surprises" (Radiohead)
I-V-vi-IV	"With or Without You" (U2) / "21 Guns" (Green Day)
V-IV-I	"Back in Black" (AC/DC) / "I Can't Explain" (The Who)
i-iv-v	"Miss You" (The Rolling Stones) / "Losing My Religion" (R.E.M)
ii-V-I	"Satin Doll" (Duke Ellington) / "Summertime" (George Gershwin)
i-VII-VI	"All Along the Watchtower" (Bob Dylan)

Cʜᴏʀᴅ ᴘʀᴏɢʀᴇssɪᴏɴs don't necessarily have to begin on the I chord either. The V-IV-I (**FIGURE 103**), which is traditionally played in blues turnarounds, has also been used as the main chord progression for many classic rock songs such as "Sweet Home Alabama" by Lynyrd Skynyrd and "Back in Black" by AC/DC. This type of descending chord pattern is also known as a *cadence*. Not surprisingly, the often used "Jazz Progression" is a staple of jazz music and another cadential pattern that begins on the ii and then moves to the V and I chords (**FIGURE 104**). It can be heard in dozens of jazz standards including "Summertime" and "Honeysuckle Rose."

Figure 103 - *V-IV-I Progression in G*

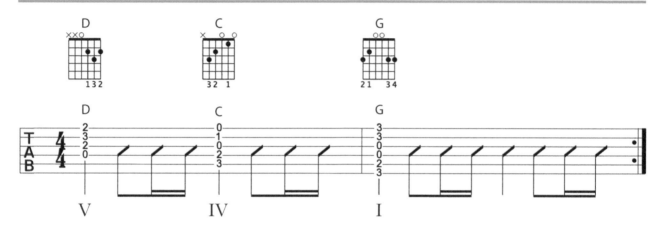

Figure 104 - *ii-V-I Progression in C*

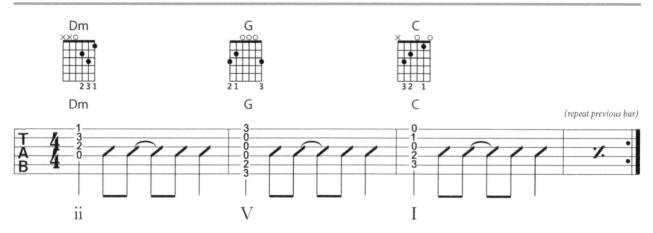

THUS FAR, WE'VE LOOKED mainly at popular chord progressions that have been in a major key. If you start on the 6th degree of the major scale, you are now in a relative minor key, meaning that while the notes and chords are the same, the tonal center now revolves around the minor chord, e.g., the relative minor key for C major (C-D-E-F-G-A-B) is A minor (A-B-C-D-E-F-G). The formula is now changed to 1=minor, 2=diminished, 3=major, 4=minor, 5=minor, 6=major, 7=major. **FIGURE 105** is an example of changing the major I-IV-V progression into a minor i-iv-v progression. Examples of this can be heard in "I Shot the Sheriff" by Bob Marley (i-iv-i) and "Losing My Religion" by R.E.M. (i-v). Our last progression (**FIGURE 106**) is a descending i-VII-VI pattern heard in "All Along the Watchtower" by Bob Dylan and the ending of Led Zeppelin's "Stairway to Heaven."

Figure 105 - *i-iv-v Progression in Am*

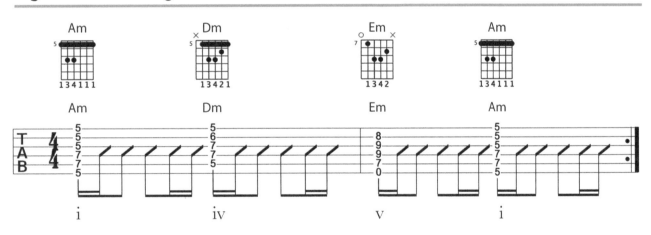

Figure 106 - *i-VII-VI Progression in Bm*

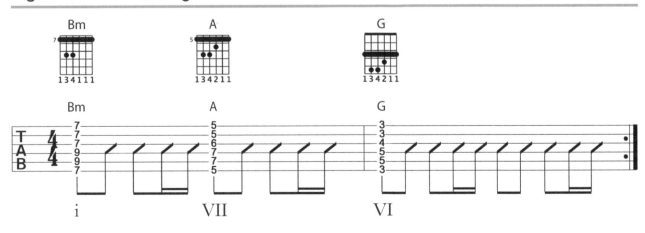

LESSON 20

GUITAR SOLOS

A guitar solo is a single-note instrumental passage or section of a song that is often improvised but can also be very melodic. The solo examples in this lesson utilize some common soloing techniques that can be applied to various styles of music.

E MINOR PENTATONIC SCALE

MOST OF THE GUITAR SOLOS that you listen to are based on the *pentatonic scale*. Unlike the major scale, the pentatonic contains only five notes and gets its name from the Latin words *penta* meaning five, and *tonic*, which refers to the notes or tones. Just like major and minor scales, there is also a major and minor pentatonic scale. We'll focus on the minor pentatonic as it is the most widely used of the two scales, beginning with the E minor pentatonic in the open-position (**FIGURE 107**).

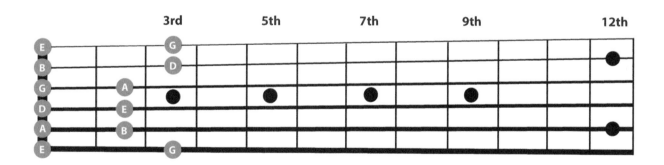

Figure 107 - *E Minor Pentatonic Scale*

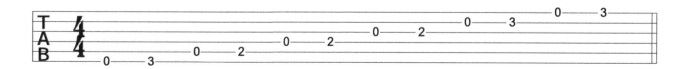

PHRASING

A GOOD GUITAR SOLO should try to convey something to the listener, rather than sounding like a bunch of meaningless notes. Phrasing is similar to speech in that a wide range of emotions can be expressed depending on the tone, dynamics, and note choice. The example in **FIGURE 108** is a common pentatonic phrase that can be repeated and expanded upon using the other notes of the scale (**FIGURE 109**).

Figure 108

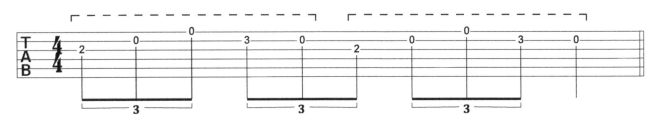

Figure 109

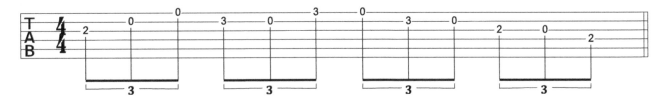

▶ TRACK LIST	Essential Guitar Solos
"Eruption"	Eddie Van Halen (Van Halen)
"Crossroads"	Eric Clapton (Cream)
"Heartbreaker"	Jimmy Page (Led Zeppelin)
"November Rain"	Slash (Guns N' Roses)
"Comfortably Numb"	David Gilmour (Pink Floyd)
"Voodoo Child (Slight Return)"	Jimi Hendrix
"Sultans of Swing"	Mark Knopfler (Dire Straits)
"Crazy Train"	Randy Rhoads (Ozzy Ozbourne)
"Johnny B. Goode"	Chuck Berry
"Texas Flood"	Stevie Ray Vaughn

ARTICULATION

ARTICULATION TECHNIQUES such as string bending can add a lot of flavor to a solo, giving you a wider range of expressive possibilities (**FIGURE 110**). Hammer-ons and pull-offs are useful in that they allow you to connect the notes more smoothly and make it easier to play faster. (**FIGURE 111**).

Figure 110

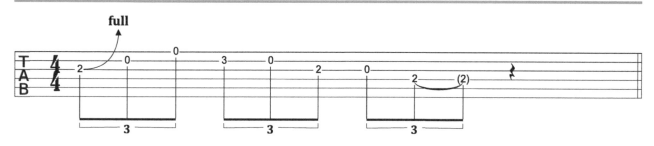

Figure 111

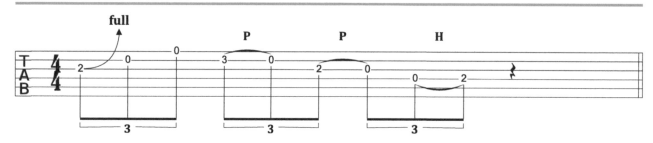

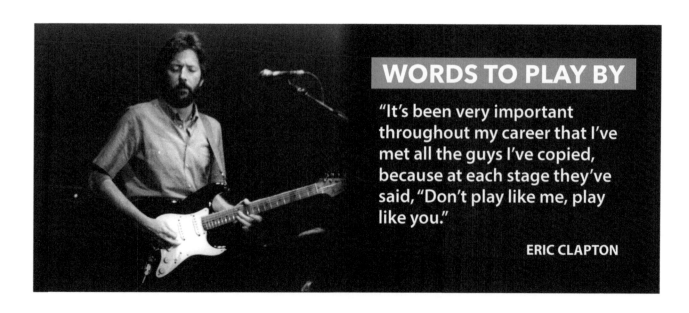

WORDS TO PLAY BY

"It's been very important throughout my career that I've met all the guys I've copied, because at each stage they've said, "Don't play like me, play like you."

ERIC CLAPTON

THE PENTATONIC BOX PATTERN

THE A MINOR PENTATONIC SCALE is located in the fifth-position, meaning that the index finger is aligned with the fifth fret (**FIGURE 112**). This particular scale pattern is frequently called a "box" pattern as it has a span of only four frets, keeping the scale tones in one convenient area. **FIGURES 113-114** are ascending and descending triplet phrases played in a repeated pattern called a *sequence*, another useful soloing device.

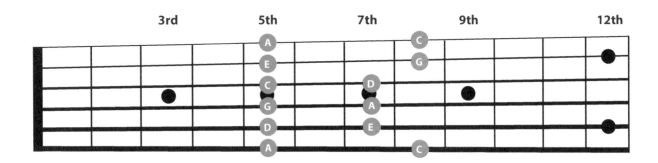

Figure 112 - *A Minor Pentatonic Scale*

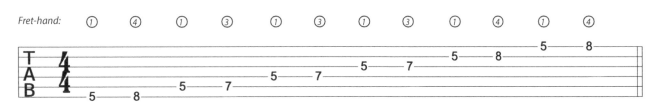

Figure 113

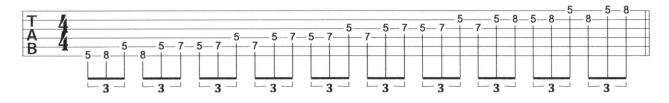

Figure 114

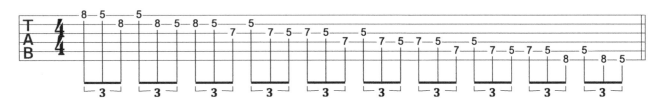

VIBRATO

ANOTHER ARTICULATION TECHNIQUE that you can utilize is *vibrato*. The effect is achieved by bending the string up and down in short, rapid movements creating a "warbling" sound (**FIGURES 115-116**).

Figure 115

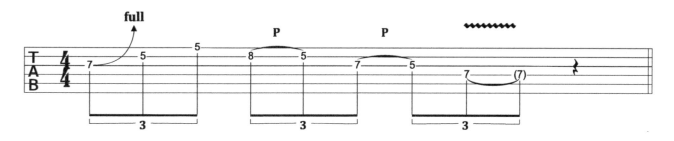

Figure 116

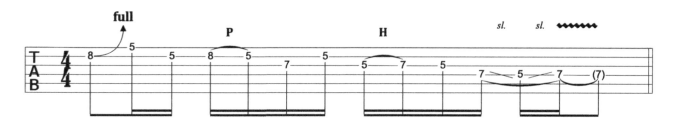

PRACTICE TIP!

Wrapping the thumb

When playing bends, wrap your thumb around the neck, "squeezing" the string up using your middle finger for extra support.

REPEATED LICKS

THE LAST TECHNIQUE that we'll look at is *repeated licks.* Repeated licks can build intensity in a solo and generally consist of three to four notes played in an equally spaced rhythmic pattern. The examples in **FIGURES 117-119** are some common repeated licks that are based on a eighth-note triplet. To ensure accuracy, barre the 1st and 2nd strings with your index finger, keeping it firmly in place while the ring finger plays the other notes.

Figure 117

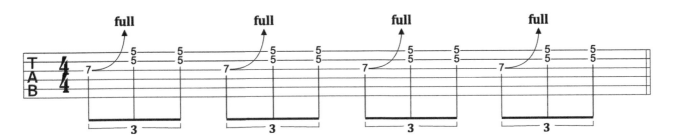

Figure 118

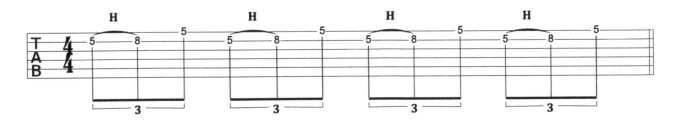

Figure 119

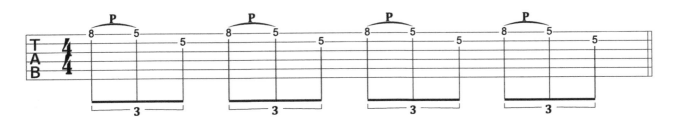

PART FOUR

HELPFUL
RESOURCES

FRETBOARD DIRECTORY

OPEN CHORDS

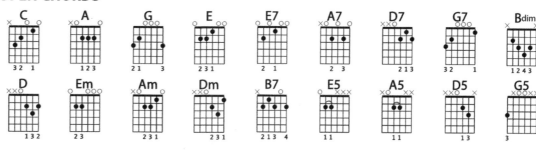

FRETBOARD NOTES

BARRE CHORDS

Sixth-String-Root

Fifth-String-Root

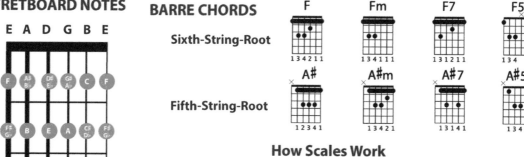

How Scales Work

The musical alphabet contains seven *natural notes* that move in a cyclical pattern. Ascending: A, B, C, D, E, F, G, A, B, C *etc*. Descending: G, F, E, D, C, B, A, G, F *etc*. Between the natural notes are accidentals called *sharps* and *flats*. Sharps raise the pitch of a note by a half step (one fret up), while flats lower the pitch by a half step. The distance between two notes is called an *interval*. The chromatic scale is a twelve note pattern of half step intervals:

A-A#-B-C-C#-D-D#-E-F-F#-G-G#

Major Scale

The major scale (do-re-mi-fa-so-la-ti-do) is a seven note scale that is made up of a repeated pattern of whole step (two frets up) and half step intervals: W-W-H-W-W-W-H.

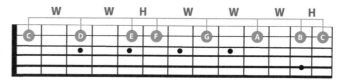

Minor Scale

The relative minor scale contains the same notes as the major scale with the tonal center starting on the 6th scale degree.

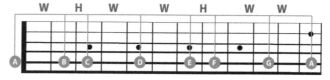

Minor Pentatonic Scale

Pentatonic scales are composed of only five notes. The minor pentatonic removes the 2nd and 6th scale degree of the minor scale.

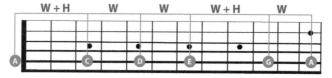

STRUM PATTERNS

NOTATION KEY

whole note = 4 beats   half note = 2 beats   quarter note = 1 beat   eighth note = 1/2 beat   sixteenth note = 1/4 beat

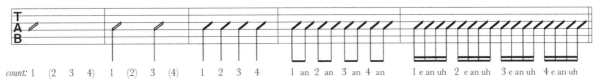

count: 1 (2 3 4)   1 (2) 3 (4)   1 2 3 4   1 an 2 an 3 an 4 an   1 e an uh 2 e an uh 3 e an uh 4 e an uh

COMMON RHYTHMS

1   2   3   an   4   an

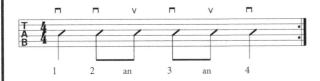

1   2   an   3   an   4

1   2   an   3   4   an

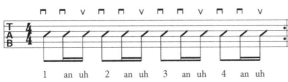

1 an uh   2 an uh   3 an uh   4 an uh

1 e an   2 e an   3 e an   4 e an

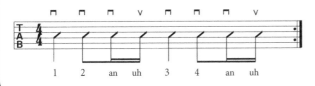

1   2   an   uh   3   4   an   uh

SYNCOPATED RHYTHMS

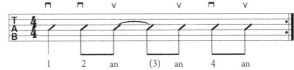

1   2   an   (3) an   4   an

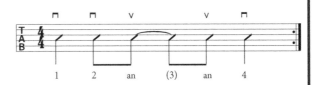

1   2   an   (3) an   4

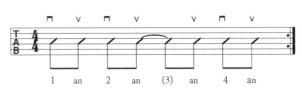

1   an   2   an   (3) an   4   an

SHUFFLE RHYTHM

1 (an) uh   2 (an) uh   3 (an) uh   4 (an) uh

⊓ = *downstroke*   V = *upstroke*

KEY CHART

	I	ii	iii	IV	V	vi	vii°
Key of C	C	D	E	F	G	A	B
Key of G	G	A	B	C	D	E	F♯
Key of D	D	E	F♯	G	A	B	C♯
Key of A	A	B	C♯	D	E	F♯	G♯
Key of E	E	F♯	G♯	A	B	C♯	D♯
Key of B	B	C♯	D♯	E	F♯	G♯	A♯
Key of F♯/ G♭	F♯/ G♭	G♯/ A♭	A♯/ B♭	B	C♯/ D♭	D♯/ E♭	E♯/ F
Key of D♭	D♭	E♭	F	G♭	A♭	B♭	C
Key of A♭	A♭	B♭	C	D♭	E♭	F	G
Key of E♭	E♭	F	G	A♭	B♭	C	D
Key of B♭	B♭	C	D	E♭	F	G	A
Key of F	F	G	A	B♭	C	D	E

HOW IT WORKS

A *key* is comprised of the notes from the major scale. The chords are created by stacking every other note on top of each other. Major, minor, and diminished chords have three notes, e.g. C major: C-E-G, Am: A-C-E etc. This creates a chord pattern labeled with Roman numerals that is the same for every key. The key chart above shows the relationship of the chords for each key.

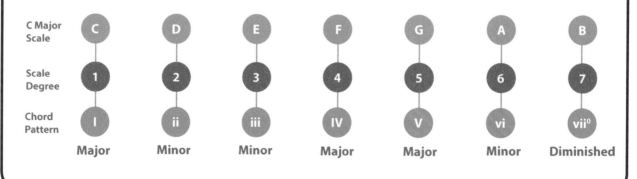

CHORD CONSTRUCTION

CHORD TYPE	SYMBOL	FORMULA	EXAMPLE
Major	M or maj	1 - 3 - 5	C - E - G
Minor	m or min	1 - ♭3 - 5	C - E♭ - G
Diminished	o or dim	1 - ♭3 - ♭5	C - E♭ - G♭
Augmented	+ or aug	1 - 3 - #5	C - E - G#
Major 7th	maj 7 or M7	1 - 3 - 5 - 7	C - E - G - B
Minor 7th	min 7 or m7	1 - ♭3 - 5 - ♭7	C - E♭ - G - B♭
Dominant 7th	7	1 - 3 - 5 - ♭7	C - E - G - B♭
Minor 7th ♭5 (half diminished)	-7 ♭5, m7♭5, or °7	1 - ♭3 - ♭5 - ♭7	C - E♭ - G♭ - B♭
Diminished 7	dim 7 or °7	1 - ♭3 - ♭5 - ♭♭7	C - E♭ - G♭ - B♭♭
Augmented 7	aug7, +7 , or 7 #5	1 - 3 - #5 - ♭7	C - E - G# - B♭
Add 9	add 9	1 - 3 - 5 - 9	C - E - G - D*
Suspended 2nd	sus 2	1 - 2 - 5	C - D - G
Suspended 4th	sus or sus 4	1 - 4 - 5	C - F - G
Power Chord	5	1 - 5	C - G

*octave above

HOW IT WORKS

Chords are created by stacking the 1st, 3rd, and 5th scale degrees and is called a *triad*. The distances between the scale degrees are often referred to as "thirds". A "minor 3rd" is one-and-a-half-steps or three frets up, while a "major 3rd" is two steps or four frets. When the triad is modified it is notated. For example, minor chords are created by lowering the third scale degree of the major triad by a half step and are written with a lower case "m" next to the letter name. To make a seventh chord, you simply add the seventh degree of the major scale. You can also replace, or suspend, the third with the second or fourth scale degree to create a suspended chord.

C Major Chord

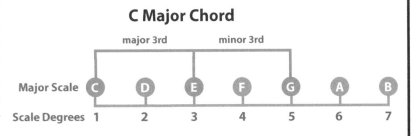

C Minor Chord

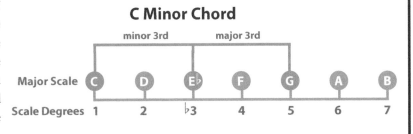

GLOSSARY

ACOUSTIC GUITAR
A nylon or steel-stringed guitar that has a hollow body.

ACCIDENTAL
Symbol used to raise or lower a note's pitch.

ALTERNATE PICKING
A picking technique that involves the strict use of downward and upward strokes.

ARPEGGIO
A music technique where the notes in a chord are played in a sequence, one at a time.

BARRE CHORD
A chord shape that involves the use of the index finger to press down on all six strings.

BASS STRUM
A strum style where a bass note is plucked and followed by a strum.

BRIDGE
A device used to support the strings on the body of the guitar.

CHORD
A group of notes sounded at the same time.

CHORD PROGRESSION
A series of chords played in a musical sequence.

CHROMATIC SCALE
Musical scale consisting of twelve pitches a half step apart.

COMPING
An abbreviation for accompanying, comping refers to a chord pattern played underneath an improvised melody or solo.

DIATONIC CHORDS
Chords that belong to the same key and share the same notes.

ECONOMY PICKING
A picking technique where the picking motion changes with the direction of the string changes.

ELECTRIC GUITAR
A type of guitar that uses electronics to amplify the sound.

FLAT
A symbol($\flat$) used to indicate the lowering of a note by a half step.

FRET
A metal strip placed across the fretboard.

GALLOP RHYTHM
A type of beat or rhythm that resembles the sound of a galloping animal.

HAMMER-ON
A technique where a note is sounded by "hammering" the finger onto the fretboard.

HEADSTOCK
The uppermost portion of the guitar used to mount the tuning pegs.

KEY
The major or minor scale that a piece of music revolves around.

MAJOR SCALE
A seven note scale consisting of a repeated pattern of whole steps and half steps: w-w-h-w-w-w-h.

MEASURE
The space where notes are written and organized. Also referred to as a *bar*.

MELODY
A sequence of notes that is rhythmically organized to express a theme or idea.

NUT
String support located near the headstock.

OCTAVE
A large interval of eight scale degrees.

OPEN CHORD
A type of chord that includes one or more open strings.

PALM MUTING
A technique where the strings are muted with the picking hand.

PEDAL TONE
A note that is sustained while the other notes in the sequence change.

PENTATONIC SCALE
A scale consisting of five notes.

PICK
A small, flat tool used to pluck or strum the strings. Also referred to as a *plectrum*.

POSITION
A fixed location on the fretboard where each finger is assigned a specific fret.

POWER CHORDS
A chord that consists of only the root and fifth.

PULL-OFF
A technique where a note is sounded by "pulling" on the string with the fretting hand.

REST
A duration of silence.

RIFF
A repeated melodic phrase that can also serve as an accompaniment.

ROOT
The note from which a chord is built.

SEVENTH CHORD
A chord that consists of a triad with an added seventh scale degree.

SHARP
A symbol (♯) used to indicate the raising of a note by a half step.

SLIDE
A technique where the next note is produced by sliding up or down the string.

SOUNDHOLE
A circular opening on an acoustic guitar used to project sound.

STANDARD TUNING
A type of tuning where the string pitches are tuned low to high: E-A-D-G-B-E.

STRING BENDING
A technique where the next note is produced by pushing or pulling the string to a desired pitch.

SYNCOPATION
A rhythmic pattern characterized by offbeats.

TABLATURE
A notation system for stringed instruments that indicates the placement of the fingers to the strings and frets.

TEMPO
The speed of a piece of music.

TIE
A curved line that connects two notes together, indicating that the first note is played while the second note rings out.

TIME SIGNATURE
A musical symbol that designates the number of beats per measure and their value.

TUNING PEG(S)
A device located on the headstock used to hold and tune the string.

TURNAROUND
A musical passage at the end of a section that leads to the beginning of the section.

```
T
A
B
```

```
T
A
B
```

```
T
A
B
```

```
T
A
B
```

```
T
A
B
```

```
T
A
B
```

```
T
A
B
```

```
T
A
B
```

```
T
A
B
```

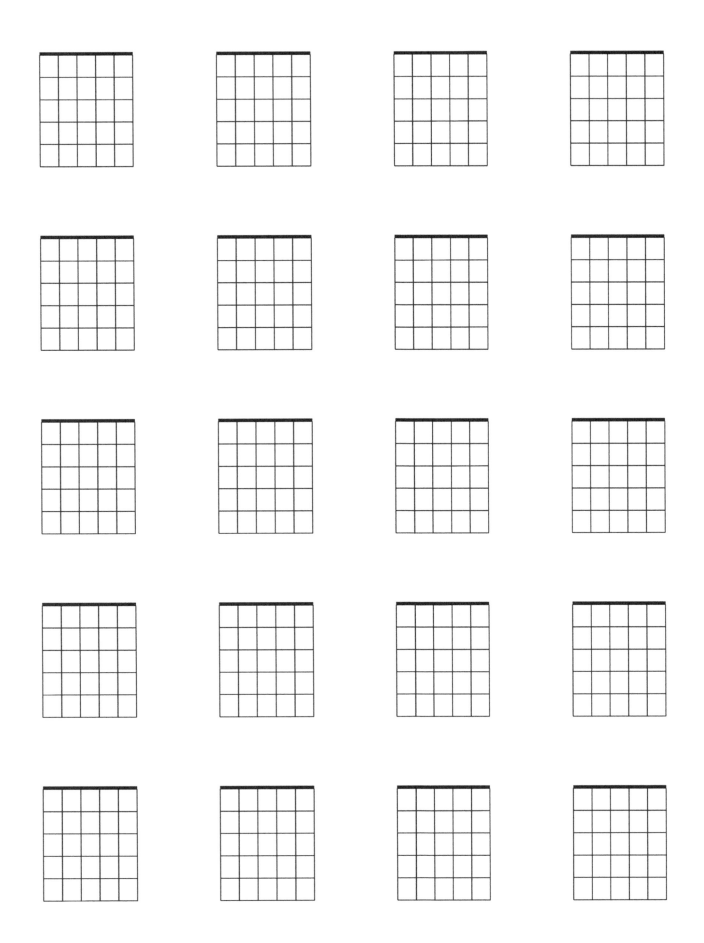

NOTATION LEGEND

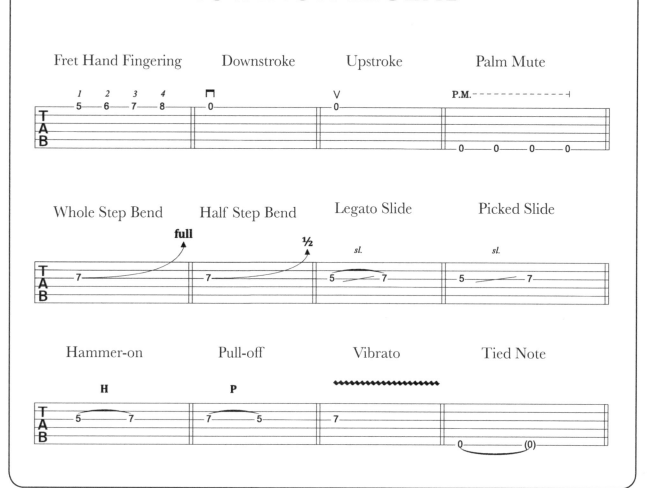

To view and download the lesson videos go to:
GuitarRoads.com/book-downloads

CPSIA information can be obtained at www.ICGtesting.com
Printed in the USA
BVOW10s1741260315

393389BV00007B/8/P

9 780991 549207